CHARLES I AND HIS EARLIER PARLIAMENTS

CHARLES I AND HIS EARLIER PARLIAMENTS

A VINDICATION
AND A CHALLENGE

BY

HAROLD P. COOKE, M.A.,

sometime Lecturer in the University of Durham; author of
" Osiris, a Study in Myths, Mysteries and Religion."

" Then came silence, then a voice,
Monotonous and hollow like a Ghost's,
Denouncing judgment, but tho' changed, the King's."
—TENNYSON, *Guinevere.*

" England can never be ruined but by her Parliament."
—BURGHLEY.

LONDON
THE SHELDON PRESS
NORTHUMBERLAND AVENUE, W.C. 2
NEW YORK: THE MACMILLAN COMPANY

First published 1939

Made in Great Britain

CONTENTS

PRINCIPAL CONTEMPORARY EVIDENCE CITED

Journals of the House of Lords. Vol. III. Cited as Lords' Journals (L.J.).

Journals of the House of Commons. Vol. I. Cited as Commons' Journals (C.J.).

Bibliotheca Regia, or The Royall Library. London, 1659.

Reliquiae Sacrae Carolinae. Hague, N.D.

Debates in the House of Commons in 1625. Ed. S. R. Gardiner. Printed for the Camden Society. 1873. Cited as Fawsley Debates, and so cited in his History by Gardiner.

State Papers, Domestic Series, 1623–5, 1625–6, 1628–9. Usually cited as S.P.D.

Buccleugh MSS. Vol. I. Historical MSS. Commission.

Coke MSS. Vol. I. Historical MSS. Commission.

Hacket, J. *Scrinia Reserata.* London, 1693.

Rous, J., Diary of (1625–42). Ed. M. A. E. Green. Camden Society. 1856.

Archbishop Laud, Autobiography of. Oxford, 1839.

Eliot, Sir John. *Negotium Posterorum.* See p. 68, n. 140, *infra.*

Clarendon, Edward, Earl of. *The History of the Rebellion and Civil Wars in England.* Vol. I. Oxford, 1849.

Rushworth, J. *Historical Collections* (1618–29). London, 1659.

Select Statutes and Other Constitutional Documents, 1558–1625. Ed. G. W. Prothero. Oxford, 1913.

N.B.—Whitelock and Ludlow, so frequently read, are, at least for this period, useless.

PREFACE

The pages that follow form a challenge to the views of established historians. I claim that the evidence adduced proves, beyond any reasonable doubt, certain vital and fundamental points. First, the King had inherited the seeds of a grave constitutional struggle. Not only, indeed, were his powers and prerogatives fiercely assailed, but the monarchy itself was at stake. There had, secondly, grown up a faction, predominant then in the Commons, who were false to their most solemn pledges and acted without shame or scruple, men utterly devoid of a tincture of honesty, of honour or of humour. Their ends justified any means, howsoever unscrupulous or reckless. Subsidies, thirdly, had always been granted at need to the Crown. Having brought the Crown into a war, having pledged it their utmost assistance, they whittled them down to a minimum, leaving the King in the lurch. This in spite of the plainest of terms in their famous address to King James—an address mutilated or ignored in the pages of our modern authorities. Still more significant —indeed, revolutionary and even anarchic—was their handling of tonnage and poundage. For these were the principal established and time-honoured sources of revenue. On their collection depended not only the fleet and its upkeep but also—let this be well noted—the maintenance of the King's household. *No tonnage and poundage, no Crown.* So they made these their principal weapons of offence in the war on the monarchy. Hence, too, they time and again shelved the bill for the tonnage and poundage. They purposed to starve the King out, thus reducing the monarchy to impotence.[1] Fourthly, the King soon detected the sinister schemes thus afoot but preserved, none the less, his good humour. The quarrel was sought by the Commons; the King did his best

[1] See the Long Parliament's proceedings, though outside the scope of this volume. They granted the tonnage and poundage " from the five and twentieth day of May, one thousand six hundred forty-one, to the fifteenth of July, next ensuing." Still the same tactics at work !

to avert it—peradventure, to his final undoing. He saw that the end must be anarchy, should the conspirators triumph; yet time after time he condescended to parley or plead with the Commons. When, however, they finally, if tacitly, voted him "a capital enemy," deserving of death, in a word, for collecting his tonnage and poundage—and mark you again that without them his household could not have subsisted—he had no alternative to breaking, consistently with self-preservation, such monstrous and sanguinary claims. From that vote we must date the Rebellion, which thus commenced long before Hotham refused Charles admission to Hull.

These are plain, unequivocal words, though I venture to think them well-weighed. For the truth should at long last be known. All the statements contained in this volume are drawn from contemporary evidence. There—or nowhere—is our basis.

I append a short note on the subject of the principal modern authorities. The reader is asked to peruse it before he proceeds to the text.

There remains the somewhat melancholy duty of acknowledging the debt that I owe to Miss Phillimore of Henley-on-Thames, now unhappily no longer with us. None laboured so much and so long, so unselfishly, in a good cause, and without her encouragement this volume had probably never been written.

H.P.C.

Cambridge, 1939.

A NOTE ON THE LEADING AUTHORITIES

WRITING once to the *Morning Post,* in a letter on the study of history, Sir Charles Firth concluded as follows : " I began by reading Carlyle's *Cromwell,* which interested me in the Civil Wars. I then read Clarendon's *History of the Rebellion,* which gave me the other side of the question. I came finally to Gardiner's history of the period, which told the whole truth without partiality or bias " (July 21, 1926). Rash as, no doubt, it may seem thus to challenge so unquestioned an authority, I confess myself wholly unable to acquiesce in this verdict on Gardiner. The reasons will appear in what follows. Should the reader, however, consider that I take up more space than is fitting in dealing with Gardiner's great work, I would ask him to bear in his mind the vast influence and weight that pertain to it. Open the *Cambridge Modern History.* We read in the preface as follows : " In bringing out the present volume, the Editors cannot but once more refer to a loss which they have suffered, together with all students of English history. It had been the hope of Lord Acton, and for a time it was ours, that the eminent historian of England under James I and Charles I, under the Commonwealth, and during the earlier part of the Protectorate, would have contributed to this work a complete summary of a period of English history to whose struggles we mainly owe the preservation of our constitutional liberties.[1] But Dr. S. R. Gardiner was only able to write for our *History* the first of the chapters undertaken by him, in which he gave proof of his close study of the connexion between English and Continental affairs. This chapter was printed in an earlier volume of this work ; those dealing with the reign of Charles I and the ensuing years have been contributed by other writers, friends

---

[1] What liberties were menaced by Charles at the time that he came to the throne?

and fellow-workers of the historian whom we have lost"
(vol. iv, p. vii). Then, again, let the reader take up that
vivacious and picturesque volume, Mr. Fletcher's *Introductory
History of England from Henry VII to the Restoration.* Let
him read the Dedicatory Epistle. " Next to you," so protests
Mr. Fletcher (by " you " Professor Pollard is intended), " my
thanks are due to our Regius Professor at Oxford, whose
knowledge of Seventeenth-Century history has never been
equalled, unless by that of our lost master, S. R. Gardiner."
But if Gardiner, himself " a descendant," as he tells us, " of
Cromwell and Ireton," [2] affords us too frequent occasion to
challenge not only his theories but (what is, in truth, more
important) his actual presentation of " facts," no general
propositions will serve, and his treatment of certain great
subjects must needs be examined at length. The same reasoning applies to John Forster. Professor Trevelyan, for instance,
in his summary *History of England,* the last of our popular
sketches, most attractive and lineal descendant of John
Richard Green's famous work, recommends at the end of each
chapter some books for our further perusal. For the period
with which I am dealing his list is made up of ten only;
among them are Gardiner's great *History* and Forster's
biography of Eliot. He might with advantage have urged us,
once lured into further inquiry by the charms of his own
English style, to resort to contemporary documents.

I may add that some readers, unfamiliar with forms of
parliamentary procedure, may feel that at times I have
followed events in the Houses too closely. I ask them, if so,
to bear with me. Not only do I want them to see and to hear,
as it were, what took place. I assure them that not otherwise
can they estimate the strength of the case. I have also
allowed the protagonists to speak for themselves in the main,
where the records enable them to do so. It seems to me not
only fairer but truer to life and to action, while it takes us back
into the past, recreating, at least in some measure, what none
can now wholly recover—an atmosphere, a world, an environ-
ment, so alien in some ways from ours. Thus it helps us to

[2] See *The Fall of the Monarchy of Charles I* (1882), I, p. vi.

realize better how bygone are now those old times, into which we must not read our own. As a rule I, however, have ventured to modify the obsolete spelling, as nothing, at least in most cases, depends on its strict preservation.

I am asking that the reader should put himself back again into the past or suppose he was now living there. He will find it, I think, fascinating.

INTRODUCTION

THOUGH many have written the history of England, some parts remain very obscure and, among them, above all, the struggle between Charles the First and the Commons. My purpose in the following pages is not to rewrite the whole story—for that would demand too much space, not to say too much labour and time—but to reconstruct some of its earlier, some of its most vital chapters in the light of the oldest authorities. Thus and thus only, I think, can we see how things looked at the time, as distinct from the way they looked later to those who knew also the sequel. We cannot be fair to the actors unless we can look through their eyes, without seeing what they neither saw nor so much as had dimly conjectured. To appreciate the course of events we must needs bring a much sharper vision but one that is much more contracted. Their work has borne fruits of a kind which the world may now call good or evil. Opinions on that point will differ. But this may be safely asserted : the fruits, whatsoever they may be, were neither foreseen nor intended. Moreover, we falsify history by reading it, so to speak, backwards and reading what never was there.

We, moreover, in dealing with the struggle between Charles the First and the Commons, propose to inquire into *causes*. And these we shall hardly discover by plunging *in medias res* or by passing in rapidity over the very first years of the reign or, in truth, the first months, the first weeks. These are vital to any such purpose. We must go to the very beginning, to find there the roots of the matter. And so let us carefully examine the doings of Charles's first parliament, bearing in mind the main question, " Which side was it opened hostilities? Which declared war on the other? " Perhaps we shall see in due course and apportion praise and blame more correctly.

CHAPTER I

THE YOUNG KING IN REAL LIFE

BUT first let us turn to the palace. The reader is shortly to see the young King face to face with the Houses. What manner of man was the sovereign in his private, more intimate life? We may now and then catch a brief glimpse in some letter from well-informed quarters. "The King shows himself in every way very gracious and affable; but the Court is kept more strict and private than in the former time. He is very attentive and devout at prayers and sermons, gracing the preachers and assembly with amiable, cheerful countenance, which gives much satisfaction: and there is great hope conceived that the world will every way amend, if the necessities of the time constrain not the contrary now at the first." [1] So Chamberlain wrote in a letter intended for Carleton's eyes only, not knowing that "now at the first" there were those for "constraining the contrary," numerous and powerful enough soon to bring all such hopes to the ground. Shortly after "some great ones" at Court wanted Anglesey, known as Kit Villiers, again to be sworn of the chamber; but the King would have none of your "drunkards." [2] He loved state and order at Court but at times could be "merry" and "jocund," as when he came up from Gravesend with the Queen before parliament opened. [3] He spoke of himself as no orator, he wished to be known by his deeds, and there seems little doubt that he suffered from some "imperfection of speech," upon which we shall shortly say more. None the less, he was clear and concise and could turn a neat phrase on occasion. [4] His

[1] *Court and Times of Charles the First,* I, p. 8 ; April 9, 1625.
[2] Mead to Stuteville, *Court and Times of Charles the First,* I, p. 12 ; April 23, 1625.
[3] Tobie Matthew to Carleton, *State Papers, Domestic Series,* 1625, 1626, p. 10 ; *Court and Times of Charles the First,* I, p. 31.
[4] See his speeches in opening parliament in this and the following years ; also Mead to Stuteville, *Court and Times,* I, p. 81.

interests were many and diverse. He hunted or rode " almost daily," lost money and games, playing tennis.[5] When Laud was at Windsor his table-talk turned upon points of philosophy.[6] His taste in fine art was supreme, and of painters and paintings few monarchs, few popes can have been better judges. I do not say patrons but *judges,* though Charles was himself a great patron. No European court in those days was so brilliant, so humane, so grave. He was not without faith in himself, neither lacking at times in high spirits. As he gazed on a much troubled world from his quiet college windows at Christ's, had not Mead some good stories to tell for Sir Martin's particular benefit? " The Dunkirkers lately took three of our merchants' ships, which the Spanish Leiger came presently to excuse to our new King, offering full satisfaction to a penny. The King answered, he desired none but should find time to make himself amends." [7] The Spaniard must write something home of the great English fleet then preparing. " As an answer from his Majesty, the King bade him write this—that his sister has now a King to her brother." [8] Charles had, too, a certain grave modesty, being, as he said, " a young man," who might well from inexperience in the past have been drawn into great schemes too rashly.[9] But weakness was not in his nature. D'Ewes wrote in the following summer (he, too, corresponded with Stuteville), " Certainly he will never yield to the Duke's [that is, Buckingham's] fall, being a young man, resolute, magnanimous and tenderly and firmly affectionate where he takes." [10]

At one time his life was despaired of, and all James's children were sickly. But now, save in one respect only, he lacked no exterior qualities. " In his childhood he was noted

[5] Mead to Stuteville, *Court and Times,* I, p. 49 ; *S.P.D.,* 1625, 1626, p. 577.
[6] *Autobiography of Archbishop Laud* (1839), p. 44.
[7] *Court and Times,* I, p. 6.
[8] *Ibid.,* I, p. 12.
[9] See p. 169, *infra.*
[10] *Court and Times,* I, p. 101. Forster attributes this letter to " the gossiping Mede " *(Sir John Eliot,* I, p. 552). The context does not make it clear whether d'Ewes here expresses his own or is quoting Robert Cotton's opinion.

to be very wilful, somewhat inclining to a perverseness of disposition, which might proceed from that retiredness, which the imperfection of his speech, not fitting him for public discourse, and the weakness of his limbs and joints (as unfit for action) made him most delight in. But now being grown both in years and state, he began to shake off that retiredness and betake himself to all manner of manlike exercises; such as were vaulting, riding great horses, running at the ring, shooting in crossbows, muskets and sometimes in great pieces of ordnance, in which he became so perfect, that he was thought to be the best marksman, and the most comely manager of a great horse of any one in all three kingdoms. And as he shaked off this retiredness, so he corrected in himself the peccancy of that humour which had grown up with it; there being no man to be found of an evener temper, more pliant to good counsel, or less wedded than he was to his own opinion." [11] I commend this account to the reader; it strikes one as speaking the truth. There is nothing of flattery in it; its terms are precise and detailed.

There remained, as we saw, still some defect that made public speaking a burden. To this, whatsoever it was, Charles appears to have freely alluded; " unfit for much speaking," " no orator," such were his own candid words.[12] This explained, too, his speaking by Williams after opening the parliament in June; but it placed him at some disadvantage, compared with the men in the Commons that now were " constraining the contrary " and led each assault on the Crown.

Such then are the glimpses we have of the King in his twenty-fifth year. Nearly forty years after this date said, of

[11] *Reliquiae Sacrae Carolinae,* p. 8. My copy of this valuable volume was published without any date but can hardly from internal evidence be later than 1660 or before 1654. The writer refers to " his childhood." It is plain he could not have invented the defect to which he refers. As to whether the King overcame it, he does not explicitly say. His silence is, however, significant, and Charles's own words seem decisive for these early years of his reign. Then again, those who trouble to study the contemporary reports of his trial must, I think, become painfully aware that the answers ascribed to the King can only be those of a man who was suffering from some such impediment.

[12] See, for instance, p. 170, *infra.*

all men, the regicide, Cook, " He was as gracious and wise a prince as any was in the world." [13]

If, as Froude has observed in his *Caesar*,[14] " our characters are written in our forms, and the bust of Cicero is the key to his history," the reader might well do far worse than examine Mytens' portrait of Charles, which was painted about four years later. The face is, though long, well-proportioned; the features are striking, yet regular. The forehead is high, the brows arched, while the nose is at once large and thin. Both the eyes and the eyelids are prominent, the expression concentrated and serious. The lips are a little compressed, and the lower unusually full, while the chin is both clear-cut and firm. The moustache is the same as Vandyck's, but the beard is more pointed and smaller. The neck is, of course, not exposed but does not, as I think, suggest weakness.

At the time of his coming to the throne Charles was not ill-disposed towards parliaments. When Prince, he was also a peer, and his frequent attendance in the Lords may be seen in the pages of the *Journals*. In the March of the previous year we find Chamberlain reporting to Carleton that the Prince " attends Parliament daily, and watches so carefully over affairs that all the good that results will be owing to him; he is free from all vicious inclinations, his actions gracious and graceful, and his journey to Spain has much improved him." [15] At the same time young Carleton was writing that " Parliament is fitful and does little, though the Prince and Duke try to settle a better understanding between it and the King." [16] One or two minor points deserve notice. That famous address was preparing, to which we shall often recur, but then ran in the name of the Commons. To this the Lords raised an objection. At a conference between the two Houses the Prince took his stand

---

[13] *An Exact and most Impartial Accompt of the Indictment, Arraignment, Trial and Judgment (according to Law) of Twenty Nine Regicides* (1679), p. 145.
[14] p. 541.
[15] *State Papers Domestic*, 1623–5, p. 193.
[16] *Ibid.*, p. 191.

by the wording. The grant, he said, came from the Commons; except out of courtesy only, they need not " acquaint the Lords with it." [17] This certainly showed some respect for the privileges—or claims—of the Commons. Moreover, it proves that the Prince had devoted some attention to precedents and studied parliamentary procedure. Again, in the following May it was due to his own mediation that sittings were prolonged for a week, although James was reluctant to yield.[18] If Clarendon knew aught about it, James roundly rebuked these proclivities and, " turning in some anger to the prince, told him, ' That he would live to have his bellyful of parliaments : and that when he should be dead, he would have too much cause to remember, how much he had contributed to the weakening of the crown, by this precedent he was now so fond of ' ; intending as well the engaging the parliament in the war, as the prosecution of the Earl of Middlesex." [19] Clarendon cannot be relied on in dealing with these early years ; but " his bellyful " seems no invention, however he came by the story—a question we cannot determine. The theory that Charles in his youth claimed an absolute power for the Crown, had extravagant notions of kingship, was antipathetic to parliament, seems, in my judgement at least, to be open to the gravest suspicion. I know of no evidence for it, and what we have cited goes against it. The burden of proof lies on those, Whigs or Tories, who bring up that charge. I believe he sought appeasement and ensued it, desiring " a better understanding." James may have seen the dissensions that soon would rend England in twain. But if Charles had more faith and less prescience, nothing could well be more likely in one of his immature years.

The Prince enjoyed wide popularity. Six months before his accession he, so we are told in a letter, " is not yet recovered of his fall ; there is great tenderness shown towards him, and there were bells and bonfires on the 5th, the

[17] *Ibid.*, p. 196.
[18] *Ibid.*, pp. 251, 252, 254.
[19] *History of the Rebellion and Civil Wars in England* (1849), I, p. 32.

anniversary of his return from Spain." [20]   We shall quote a
few words from John Rous.[21]   But few princes have troubled
so little to win or retain popularity. A prince, too, of excellent
parts—was there anyone found to deny it? To play certain
parts, notwithstanding, he seems to have lacked skill or taste.

Most pacific of all England's princes—the Stuarts were
pacific by nature—King James had neglected the navy. Not
so did his youthful successor. He no sooner mounted the
throne than he issued a proclamation " for better furnishing
the navy with skilful mariners." [22]   Nor was he content with
such measures. When he made his first public appearance,
he paid a state visit to Blackwall and held a review of the
fleet. How near was the fleet to his heart we shall see more
than once in these pages. And now that it was fitting in the
Thames for important operations at sea, the young King must
go down and inspect and encourage the enterprise in person,
not unlike his predecessor, Elizabeth, in that, if no other,
respect.[23]

Just a word of the King's chief advisers. Chamberlain
wrote thus to Carleton : " We talk of a selected or cabinet
council [how old is that phrase ' cabinet council ' !], whereto
none are admitted but the Duke of Buckingham, Lord
Treasurer [Ley], Lord Chamberlain [Pembroke], Lord Brooke,
and the Lord Conway, who, they say, will leave his place and
go for Ireland, when this bottom is untwined they are now
about." These five were the same Privy Councillors
appointed in April by Charles to consider certain articles of
state.[24] Tobie Matthew had also told Carleton that Buckingham stands " hugely high in the substantial part of the King's
favour," while Conway is " the greatest instrument in the
despatch of business " and " after the Duke the King hears
no counsellors so gladly as the Lord Treasurer and the Lord
Chamberlain." [25]   That Buckingham held a great place not

---

[20] Chamberlain to Carleton, October 9 ; S.P.D., 1623–5, p. 352.
[21] See p. 17, infra.
[22] S.P.D., p. 31 ; March 31.
[23] Meddus to Meade, April 22 ; Court and Times, I, p. 11.
[24] Court and Times, I, p. 14 ; S.P.D., p. 7.
[25] S.P.D., p. 10, April 17.

only in the King's estimation but also in his personal affections no competent student would deny.   To go further and suppose that the King, in plain language, was not his own master would be lacking, so far as I can see, in support from reliable evidence.   Therefore Ley, Conway, Brooke, Pembroke still less were the rulers of England.   This " closet," " selected," " cabinet council " was not what was called the Privy Council.   It might be compared in some sort with the modern so-called " inner cabinet."   In regard to the Privy Council proper, it deserves some attention in passing that no Roman Catholics were included.

Such, then, is the portrait of the King on his coming to the throne of his fathers—a portrait, at least, as " authentic " as any we can paint from the records.   I make no pretence in these pages to vie with impressionist pigments, more fit for historical novels, for satires or party propaganda.

CHAPTER II

Here, in justice to King Charles himself, I must touch on a number of points where historians, if I mistake not, have gone very sadly astray. Take, for instance, what Gardiner remarks of the King's "reserve," "reticence," "silence." Suppose that this charge was well-founded. I mentioned some defect in speaking. Was Gardiner aware of this defect? I reproduce part of the portrait he paints in cold colours of Charles. "When Ville-aux-Clercs went back to France with the marriage treaty, Richelieu asked him what he thought of Charles. 'He is either an extraordinary man,' was the shrewd reply, ' or his talents are very mean. If his reticence is affected in order not to give jealousy to his father, it is a sign of consummate prudence. If it is natural and unassumed, the contrary inference may be drawn.' The extreme reserve of the young King was doubtless closely connected with that want of imaginative power which lay at the root of his faults. With all his confidence in his own thoughts, he failed to give to his ideas an expression which was satisfactory to others or even to himself. He did not like to be contradicted, and his father's rapid utterance had swept away his slow conceptions as with a torrent before he could find out what he really meant to say. The man who is too vain to bear contradiction and not sufficiently brilliant or wise to overpower it, must of necessity take refuge in silence. Unfortunately the defect which hindered Charles from being a good talker hindered him also from being a good ruler. The firm convictions of his mind were alike proof against arguments which he was unable to understand, and unalterable by the impression of passing events, which slipped by him unnoticed. The wisest of men, the most decisive of facts, were no more to him than the whistling of the storm is to the man who is seated by a warm fireside. They passed him by; or, if he heeded them at all, it was only to wonder that they did not conform to his own beneficent intentions. 'I cannot,' he said on one occasion, 'defend a bad, nor yield in a good cause.' Conscious of the purity of his own motives, he never ceased to divide mankind into two simple classes—into those who agreed with him, and those who did not; into sheep to be cherished, and goats to be rejected. Such narrowness of view was no guarantee for fixity of purpose." [1] All this, to be sure, is fantastic. If Charles, as is claimed in this passage, could not have been called " a good talker," the reason is not to be found in " a want of imaginative power " but in something less subtle, more obvious—a simple "imperfection " in speaking. In Gardiner a physical weakness masquerades as a mental defect. Nor could it surprise us in one who was placed at a certain disadvantage, if at times Charles " took refuge in silence " or appeared to be " slow " or " reserved." His " reticence " *may* have been " natural " but not as Ville-aux-Clercs intended.

What, again, shall we say of the Frenchman on whom, it seems, Gardiner relies? Ville-aux-Clercs and the Marquis d'Effiat came " ambassadors extraordinary," to deal with the French marriage settlement. The former at that time was also Henrietta Maria's secretary. Can we call him a competent witness? Did he come much in contact with Charles? I have noted an audience at Cambridge, when Charles was among the few present, and the Prince entertained him to dinner.[2] What knowledge did he gain of the Prince in a manner less formal, more intimate?

A few words may surely suffice on the saying Gardiner quoted from Laud. Let us first cite the context as well: " February 1, Sunday. I stood by the most illustrious Prince Charles, at dinner. He was then very merry, and talked occasionally on many things with his attendants. Among other things, he said that, if he were necessitated to take any particular profession of life, he could not be a lawyer, adding his reasons : 'I cannot,' he said, ' defend a bad, nor yield in

[1] *History*, V, p. 317.
[2] *S.P.D.*, 1623–5, pp. 411, 412.

a good cause.' May you ever hold this resolution and succeed
(Most Serene Prince) in matters of greater moment, for ever
prosperous!" [3] Forster, too, seized on this passage. "Was
there ever," he thus writes, "an instance of a thoroughly
obstinate man not ready and eager to say for himself what
Charles Stuart then said?" [4] This is building "a large superstructure" on what looks uncommonly like a mere *obiter
dictum,* an epigram! Who, indeed, judges a man—not to
mention a man's whole career—by a casual remark made at
table? This man, too, was twenty-four only and also that
night *making merry.* That Laud may have taken him
literally proves, I think, little or nothing. Laud probably
never relaxed. And, if Charles could have read those remarks
about "mankind," the "sheep" and the "goats," he had
probably felt that a prince would be wise to take refuge in
"silence"—not to mention historians also, who seem somewhat lacking in humour, a quality not wholly wanting in
most, if not all, of the Stuarts.

Gardiner goes also astray, as I think, on the Cottington
case. He devotes a whole page to this story and reads the
whole reign in its light: we are clearly, in consequence, bound
to examine it somewhat at length. "Almost anyone," so he
declares, "with a courtier's introduction could gain access to
James; Charles directed that no one should be admitted to
his presence without special directions from himself. Amongst
those who were thus excluded was one who might have hoped
for better treatment. Sir Francis Cottington had been
Charles's secretary when he was Prince of Wales, and had
served him faithfully in that capacity. It was, however, well
known that, having fallen sick at Madrid, he had declared
himself to be a Roman Catholic, at least till his recovery, and
that he had since protested, like Bristol, his belief that, with the
aid of the Spanish ministers, the restoration of the Palatinate
need not be despaired of. He was now not only stripped of
his official position and emoluments, but forbidden to appear

[3] *Autobiography of Archbishop Laud,* February 1, 1623.
[4] *Sir John Eliot,* I, p. 134, note.

at Court." [5]   Then Gardiner brings Clarendon to witness. And since he quotes only a part, I transcribe here the whole of the story. " And king James," the narrative runs, " was no sooner dead, and the new officers and orders made, but the profits and privileges which had used to be continued to him who had been secretary, till some other promotion, were all retrenched. And when he was one morning attending in the privy lodgings, as he was accustomed to do, one of the secretaries of state came to him, and told him, ' that it was the king's pleasure that he should no more presume to come into those rooms ' (which was the first instance he had received of the king's disfavour); and at the same instant the duke entered into that quarter. Upon which sir Francis Cottington addressed himself towards [him], and desired ' he would give him leave to speak to him ' : upon which the duke inclining his ear, moved to a window from the company, and the other told him, ' that he received every day fresh marks of his severity '; mentioned the message which had been then delivered to him, and desired only to know, ' whether it could not be in his power, by all dutiful application, and all possible service, to be restored to the good opinion his grace had once vouchsafed to have of him, and to be admitted to serve him? ' The duke heard him without the least commotion, and with a countenance serene enough, and then answered him, ' That he would deal very clearly with him; that it was utterly impossible to bring that to pass which he had proposed : that he was not only firmly resolved never to trust him, or to have to do with [him]; but that he was, and would be always, his declared enemy; and that he would do always whatever should be in his power to ruin and destroy him, and of this he might be most assured '; without mentioning any particular ground for his so heightened displeasure. The other very calmly replied to him (as he was master of an incomparable temper), ' That since he was resolved never to do him good, that he hoped, from his justice and generosity, that he would not suffer himself to gain by his loss; that he had laid out by his command so much money for jewels and pictures, which he had received : and that, in hope of his future favour, he had once presented a suit of hangings to him, which cost him 800*l.* which he hoped he would cause to be restored to him, and that he would not let him be so great a loser by him.' The duke answered, ' he was in the right; that he should the next morning go to Oliver (who was his receiver), and give him a particular account of all the money due to him, and he should presently pay him '; which was done the next morning accordingly, without the least abatement of any of his demands." [6]

Gardiner observes of this story : " Such an anecdote as this points to the special danger of the new reign so far as it was to be influenced by Buckingham. There would be no personal meanness; but whether anyone was to be treated as a friend or as an enemy would depend entirely on the accordance of his political views with those prevalent for the time at Court. There would be no largeness of mind, no readiness to hear all sides of disputed questions." [7]

" Such an anecdote " appears circumstantial; yet, I think, we must regard it with caution. There is still in existence a warrant, " granting to Sir Francis Cottington and his heirs, in fee farm, lands to the value of 400*l.* per annum." [8] Again, so Locke wrote a week later, " Lord Conway has a pension of 2,000*l.* per ann., for 21 years; Sir Edwd. Villiers, 3,000*l.* in money; Sir Francis Cottington, a grant of 400*l.* lands; these exceed the favour shewn in Sec. Morton's pension of 500*l.* per ann." [9] Thus the grant that was made to Sir Francis was apparently esteemed very handsome.

He certainly ceased to hold office and wrote to that effect from St. James's to Elizabeth, the Queen of Bohemia.[10] But " the profits," according to Clarendon, " and privileges which had used to be continued to him who had been secretary, till some other promotion, were all retrenched." " Stripped

---

[6] *History of the Rebellion,* I, p. 45.
[7] *History,* V, p. 322.
[8] *State Papers, Domestic Series,* 1625, 1626, p. 537 ; May 20, 1625.
[9] *S.P.D.,* p. 30. Chamberlain had already written of a grant of £200 yearly. Was this in addition to land? See p. 12.
[10] *Ibid.,* p. 2 ; March 30, 1625.

of his official position and emoluments," according to
Gardiner. No mention is made of the warrant. We cannot,
I imagine, determine how Clarendon came by the story (himself little more than a boy at the time of the young King's
accession). Suppose that Sir Francis informed him—of course,
at a much later date. But could anyone glean from that story
that, deprived as he was of the profits that he had from his
previous office, Sir Francis was yet compensated in the
handsomest manner for life and provision made as well for his
heirs? And, if Buckingham really had told him " that he was,
and would be always, his declared enemy; and that he would
do always whatever should be in his power to ruin and
destroy him," how came it about that a man whom the Duke
was thus bent on destroying received this large grant from the
King? Was the King thus disposed to reward in so prompt
and so handsome a way men whom Buckingham held mortal
enemies? Then, again, " he received every day fresh marks
of " the favourite's " severity." Wherein those " marks " had
consisted we cannot so much as conjecture.

But the more we look into the story, the more are we led to
suspect it. Cottington, so we are told, was excluded by
Charles from his presence. But what, let us ask, were the
facts? In the autumn of 1623 he had certainly been out of
favour. Both Chamberlain and Nicholas say so.[11] But was
he not soon received back? In the following January
Chamberlain, writing of the general election, told Carleton
that Charles had himself tried in vain to get Cottington
chosen.[12] Charles would not thus have used influence to
bring in a man he had broken with.

Not content with all this about Cottington, Clarendon has
this appendix : " And he [the Duke] was so far reconciled to
him before his death, that being resolved to make a peace with
Spain, to the end he might more vigorously pursue the war

[11] *State Papers, Domestic Series,* 1623–5, p. 94, October 11, 1623 ;
p. 119, November 25, 1623. Cottington had turned Roman Catholic or,
at least, had professed himself such for a very few days in Madrid, as,
indeed, Gardiner notes in his *History* (V, p. 102). This, perhaps, may
explain the King's attitude. Might he not think him unstable?
[12] *S.P.D.,* p. 156.

with France (to which his heart was most passionately fixed), he sent for Cottington to come to him, and after conference with him, told him, ' the king would send him ambassador thither, and that he should attend him at Portsmouth for his despatch.' " This is certainly vague as to dates but appears to refer to the period just prior to the death of the Duke in the August of 1628. I conclude this for various reasons. First, Clarendon says "before his death," which I take to mean " shortly before it." In the next place, the Duke, as we know, was at Portsmouth more than once in that August and there, of course, met with his death. And thirdly, as the tale is related, the matter proceeded no further. But, if this conclusion is right, there are certain undeniable facts that I cannot reconcile with the story. On the 17th of March in that year Sir James Bagg had been writing to Buckingham that he " has presented the Duke with four burgesships; himself for Plympton, Sir Francis Cottington for Saltash, and two blanks, Looe and Probus." [13] Would Bagg have found Cottington a seat and have called it a present to Buckingham, if Buckingham was Cottington's enemy or Cottington then out of favour? Sir Francis was also appealed to as one who had influence at Court. He was writing for a Spaniard to Conway; Lord Poulett was seeking his services both with the King and with Marlborough.[14]

I think I have now shown strong reasons for regarding this tale with due caution. Foundation in fact it may have; what foundation, if so, we know not. But to generalize from it with Gardiner about the whole tone of the Court is to build on the flimsiest basis. Moreover, the story, *as told,* is, to my mind at least, inconsistent with Buckingham's probable character. What said the Duke of himself? " I am not vindictive, nor will be an instrument to do anything by ill

---

[13] *State Papers, Domestic Series,* 1628–9, p. 24. Bagg refers to the matter again in a letter of April the 6th. The Mayor gave him Cottington's seat. As that worthy was summoned to London to answer about a press warrant, Bagg wrote to the Duke in his favour. See *ibid.,* p. 65.

[14] *Ibid.,* pp. 75, 150; April 15 and June 4. Marlborough then was Lord Treasurer.

means." [15] Why suppose that he spoke not the truth? For, whatever his faults may have been, to convict him on that score, at least, seems as hard as convicting his master.

[15] August 8, 1625, in his speech to the Houses at Christ Church. See *Fawsley Debates*, p. 101.

CHAPTER III

THE SETTING

THE first parliament summoned by Charles met on Saturday, June the 18th. Though originally summoned by the King to assemble on May the 17th, it had twice been postponed or "prorogued" on account of the marriage festivities. The Queen had now landed in England and—such in those days were royal matches—had now first set eyes on her husband, her senior by nearly ten years. Charles, who had seen her but once, as he travelled through France in disguise on his way to the court of Madrid, had espoused her by proxy in Paris. Still a girl of no more than fifteen but a daughter of Henry the Fourth, not devoid of the wit of her race, the young Henrietta Maria, who, on landing at Dover in state, was accompanied thence by the King, entered London on June the 16th under threatening and overcast skies amid loud acclamations and salvoes. The guns of the fleet at Blackwall, then the guns of the Tower thundered welcome. All the roofs of the houses were crowded. The river itself seemed alive, as they passed to Whitehall in their barge. The King himself led out the Queen, as they came in full sight of the Tower, thus the better to see and be seen, when the rain, now descending at last, drove them into their cabin again and continued for the rest of the journey. But Charles had the windows kept open to afford a better view of the Queen and to gratify the popular instinct. Nothing, it seemed, could avail to deter the great concourse of people that thronged both the banks of the Thames or diminish the universal joy. If in all that great city some few muttered "Papists" under their breath, yet the common folk paid little heed. In the young Henrietta Maria they would see but the queen and the lover, who, leaving her own kith and kin, came to dwell in a strange, foreign land.

They would make her paths pleasant and straight. As he landed at Denmark House and escorted his bride to White-hall, might not Charles augur well for his reign from a greeting so warm and spontaneous?

From two to three months had elapsed since he came in due course to the throne. James had died on the 27th March; the same day was the Prince proclaimed King. " His coming to the throne was very joyous to the well-affected but to the Papists not very welcome," wrote kindly John Rous in his diary.[1] There was at the time some wild weather. To men superstitiously minded the skies must have seemed inauspicious. We read in a letter from Cambridge, " On Wednesday King Charles was here proclaimed, and I know not what the omen of it was, but the joy of the people devoured their mourning. We had thunder the same day, presently upon the proclamation, and 'twas a cold season, but all fears and sorrows are swallowed up in joy of so hopeful a successor."

The King was at that time most anxious to meet the two Houses at once and, except for the lawyers and judges, who urged the demise of the Crown, would have summoned his father's last parliament, avoiding a general election with all the delays it involved. When the Lord Keeper Williams, moreover, was all for postponing the writs, thinking thereby to make the elections, Charles curtly rejected the proposal, if Williams himself told the truth.[2] But the plague stalked abroad in the land. Thus there perished in London alone in the week before parliament opened one hundred and sixty-five persons. Very soon all the shops would be closed, all the fairs and the like be prohibited. The streets would at noon wear an aspect suggestive of three in the morning. Not until the last days of the year was this terrible contagion to cease. If, therefore, Charles summoned the Houses, he meant they should not sit for long. Let them run no avoidable risk. But no prince could make war without money, and the Crown had

[1] *Diary of John Rous* (1625–42), p. 1.
[2] *Scrinia Reserata* (1693), II, p. 4. According to Williams, the King was concerned in the main for *the fleet*.

been drawn into war for the purpose of recovering the Palatinate. Frederick, the Elector, had married Elizabeth, daughter of James, and in 1619 he had also accepted the crown of Bohemia. The Spaniards overran the Palatinate, and he and his wife were, in consequence, exiles from both their dominions. How Charles himself viewed the position his own words will shortly explain.

For the most part the Commons came up in no mood to do very much business. Some, such as Wentworth himself, had throughout been opposed to the war. They would not only keep out of war, whether war with the Spaniards or others; they would keep out of Europe as well. And the two things were closely connected. Such men formed an insular group. The majority of members, however, came up with but two ideas only—to see priests and Jesuits banished, to vote an immediate subsidy. Mandeville says " to give somewhat," a phrase very much to the point, as the " somewhat " was like to prove little.[3] Their leaders were Phelips and Seymour with Lord Saye and Sele in the Lords. Of these men we shall shortly see more, their intrigues, machinations, deceits, often clothed in the garb of " religion." And Coke, too, the lawyer, was there, braggart, bully, if ever there was, not to mention " King Pym," as they dubbed him in days even darker than these, while behind them there loomed the more subtle, more sinister figure of Eliot, the King's most implacable foe.

THE OPENING OF PARLIAMENT

The stage was thus set for the drama, which Charles was himself now to open. His first thought again for his people, he came to Westminster by water, dispensing with much of the pomp that would normally grace such occasions, bring multitudes into the streets and augment the prevailing mortality. The peers in their robes were assembled with Buckingham foremost among them, though seldom seen now in the Lords. The Commons were summoned to the bar.

[3] *Buccleugh MSS.*, I, p. 260, " H. [Viscount] Mandeville to his brother, Lord Mountagu, at Barnwell." This letter, we note, is undated but was written on June 22. Mandeville himself was Lord President and must have known well how things stood.

The King ordered prayers to be said, while " he kneeled by the chair of estate," first removing the crown from his head. Then he briefly addressed the two Houses. Let us listen awhile to his words :

" My Lords and Gentlemen, you are not ignorant, that at your earnest entreaty, March 23, 1623, my father (of happy memory) first took up arms for the recovery of the Palatinate, for which purpose by your assistance he began to form a considerable army, and prepare a goodly armado and navy royal. But death intervening between him and the achievement, the war, with the Crown, is devolved upon me. To the prosecution whereof, as I am obliged both in nature and honour, so I question not, but the same necessity continuing, you'll cherish the action with the like affection, and further it with a ready contribution. True it is, you furnished my father with affectionate supplies, but they held no symmetry or proportion with the charge of so great an enterprise. For those your donatives are all disbursed to a penny ; and I am enforced to summon you hither to tell you that neither can the army advance, nor the fleet set forth without further aid.

" Consider, I pray you, the eyes of all Europe are defixed upon me, to whom I shall appear ridiculous, as though I were unable to outgo muster and ostentation, if you now desert me. Consider it is my first attempt, wherein if I sustain a foil, it will blemish all my future honour.

" If mine cannot, let your own reputation move you : deliver and expedite me fairly out of this war wherewith you have encumbered (let it never be said whereunto you have betrayed) me. I desire therefore your speedy supply ; speedy I call it, for else it will prove no supply. The sun, you know, is entering into his declining point, so it will be soon too late to set forth, when it will rather not be too soon to return. Again, I must remind you of the mortality now regnant in this city, which should it (as so it may, and no breach of privilege neither) arrest any one member of either House, it soon would put a period both to consultation and session ; so that your own periclitation necessitates an early resolution.

" In sum, three of the best rhetoricians, honour, oppor-

tunity, and safety, are all of a plot, and plead, you see, for
expedition. Perhaps it may be expected I should say something in way of account of my religion; as also of the temper
and tenour of my future government. But as I hope I have
not been guilty of any thing which may justly start the least
question in either; so I desire you would repose in this
assurance, that I will in neither vary from those principles
wherein I have been instituted at the feet of that eminent
Gamaliel, my late father." [4]

The King, in effect, took his stand on the Houses' address
to his father and desired them to vote him supplies in accordance with the terms of that document—that is, to keep their
pledged word, as, beyond any doubt, he conceived it. We
shall see in a moment or two what that document contained
more precisely. For there lies the root of the matter.

Williams, by his master's directions, revived a now long-
disused custom—" to have my Lord Keeper to speak for me."
No " imperfection " was his; he was facile and glib beyond
others. Describing the King's speech itself as " though short,
yet full and princely and imperatorious "—this, to be sure,
with a side-glance at James's inordinate length—he passed to
the business on hand. But naturally on such an occasion he
confined his remarks to generalities. The time for details
would come later—if only the Houses allowed it. The royal
preparations and plans centred wholly around the Palatinate.
The King would explain his " engagements." For this had he
brought them together. The subsidies voted to James had
been spent on the objects proposed, and as much more again,
for that matter, derived from the royal revenues. The
accounts they would have in due course. These, indeed, were
already drawn up and would show what was done with the
money and what would be done with any monies they
might now be willing to vote. Charles would make a clean
breast of the matter. If subsidies proved " long and backward," the King would propound no new method, though
willing and anxious to listen to any propositions put forward.
This meeting Charles asked that the Houses should devote

[4] See for this speech the appendix beginning p. 167, *infra.*

to his own urgent business; he promised the next "should be theirs and as long and as soon as they would." [5]

Then the Commons returned to their House, where they once again chose Crewe for Speaker. So ended a day fraught with issues that England had not seen the like of nor yet, we may fervently hope, may for many long days see the like. The King came again on the Monday, when the Speaker was duly presented. Crewe then reminded the King that the sword was now placed in his hands; it was his to recover the Palatinate.[6] Did Crewe speak the mind of the Commons? The King very probably thought so. The Speaker, at least, was no "courtier." His words, none the less, must have seemed like a solemn and formal endorsement of their pledges to King James, his father. Small blame if the King still assumed that the Commons, in willing the end, would still will, as they promised, the means!

THE HOUSES' ADDRESS TO KING JAMES

"At your earnest entreaty, March 23, 1623." Let us now turn at once to the document here referred to by the King. This state paper is highly important, containing, as it does, we repeat, the very heart, root or pith of the matter. It should, indeed, stand in the forefront of every account of these times. It should stand there, moreover, *complete*. It runs thus in the *House of Lords' Journals* [7] :—

"We, your Majesty's most humble and loyal subjects, the Lords and Commons in this present Parliament assembled, do first render unto your sacred Majesty our most dutiful thanks, for that, to our unspeakable comfort, you have vouchsafed to express yourself so well satisfied with our late declaration

[5] See for Williams's speech the *Lords' Journals*, III, p. 435 ; *Fawsley Debates*, p. 2 ; *Scrinia Reserata*, II, p. 9 ; also Rushworth's *Historical Collections* (1659), p. 171.   The last-named, however, in error gives the speech not to Williams but to Coventry.   Gardiner says nothing whatever about the suggested new session.

[6] *Lords' Journals*, III, p. 438.

[7] *Lords' Journals*, III, p. 275.   Buckingham appealed to this paper, when addressing the Houses at Oxford : "The first question I put to myself is :—by what counsels this great enterprise hath been undertaken and pursued hitherto?   I answer :—by the Parliament.   And then he called for a declaration, 23 March, 1623," etc.   (*Fawsley Debates*, p. 96.)

made to your Majesty, of our general resolution in pursuit of our humble advice to assist your Majesty, in a parliamentary way, with our persons and abilities.

" And whereas your Majesty, in your great wisdom and judgement, foreseeing that it would make a deeper impression both in the enemies of that cause, and in your friends and allies, if they shall not only hear of the cheerful offers, but also see the real performance of your subjects towards so great a work, your Majesty was pleased to descend to a particular proposition for the advancement of this great business.

" We, in all humbleness, most ready and willing to give your Majesty and the whole world an ample testimony of our sincere and dutiful intentions herein, have, upon mature advice and deliberation, as well of the weight and importance of this great affair, as of the present estate of this your kingdom (the weal and safety whereof is, in our judgements, apparently threatened, if your Majesty's resolution for the dissolving of the treaties now in question be longer deferred, and that provision for the defence of your realm, and aid of your friends and allies, be not seasonably made), with a cheerful consent of all the Commons (no one dissenting), and with a full and cheerful consent of us the Lords,[8] resolved : That, upon your Majesty's public declaration of the utter dissolution and discharge of the two treaties of the marriage and Palatinate, in pursuit of our advice therein, and towards the support of the war which is likely to ensue, and more particularly for those four points proposed by your Majesty, namely, the defence of this realm, the securing of Ireland, the assistance of your neighbours, the States of the United Provinces, and others your Majesty's friends and allies, and for the setting forth of your royal navy, we will grant for the present the greatest aid which was ever granted in Parliament, to be levied in so short time ; that is, three entire subsidies, and three fifteenths, to be all paid within the compass of one whole year after your Majesty shall be pleased to make the said declaration ; the money to be paid into the hands, and

[8] One peer, namely Rutland, " dissented." Charles and Buckingham failed to convert him.

expended by the direction, of such committees, or commissioners, as hereafter shall be agreed upon in this present
session of Parliament.

"And we most humbly beseech your Majesty graciously
to accept of these first fruits of our hearty oblation, dedicated
to that work which we infinitely desire may prosper and be
advanced; and for the future to rest confidently assured, that,
if you shall be engaged in a real war, we your loyal and
loving subjects will never fail to assist your Majesty, in a
parliamentary way, in so royal a design, wherein your own
honour, and the honour of your most noble son the Prince,
and the ancient renown of this nation, the welfare and very
substance of your noble and only daughter and her consort,
and their posterity, the safety of your own kingdoms and
people, and the prosperity of your neighbours and allies, are
so deeply engaged."

So runs this decisive state paper and stands for all time on
the *Journals*. Such addresses could hardly come short of
petitions and bills in their force. Let the reader mark well
the last paragraph—read and reread and digest it!

THE COMMONS' ENGAGEMENTS

What were the Commons' engagements? To what were
they solemnly *pledged?* This address, I conceive, holds the
answer, contained in their own chosen terms, to the one vital
question at issue. We must, therefore, examine it closely.
Historians too often ignore it or cite from it only such portions
as happen to suit their own views. Let us turn for a moment
to Gardiner. "The address," so he says, "from both Houses
with which this resolution [9] was accompanied plainly declared
the objects for which it was intended. They were stated to
be ' the support of the war which is likely to ensue, and more
particularly for those four points proposed by your Majesty;
namely, the defence of this realm, the securing of Ireland, the
assistance of your neighbours the States of the United

---

[9] *Commons' Journals*, I, p. 744. The objects are also set out in the
act for the grant of the subsidies; see Prothero's *Select Statutes and
Other Constitutional Documents* (1913), p. 278.

Provinces and others of your Majesty's friends and allies, and the setting forth of your Royal Navy.' " (The words that immediately precede are "upon your Majesty's public declaration of the utter dissolution and discharge of the two treaties of the marriage and Palatinate, in pursuit of our advice therein, and towards.") In his summary of James's reply, Gardiner also remarks incidentally : " In the address, the subsidies had been spoken of as ' first fruits,' and there had been a further assurance of more to come when he was actually engaged in war." [10] That is all—just one trifling allusion. Thus ends this very vital state paper : " And we most humbly beseech your Majesty graciously to accept of these first fruits of our hearty oblation, dedicated to that work which we infinitely desire may prosper and be advanced; and for the future to rest confidently assured, that, if you shall be engaged in a real war, we your loyal and loving subjects will never fail to assist your Majesty, in a parliamentary way, in so royal a design, wherein your own honour, and the honour of your most noble son the Prince, and the ancient renown of this nation, the welfare and very substance of your noble and only daughter and her consort, and their posterity, the safety of your own kingdoms and people, and the prosperity of your neighbours and allies, are so deeply engaged." [11] I repeat that the reader should read and reread and digest this plain statement.

The subsidies are, doubtless, described as "first fruits of our hearty oblation" and as granted, moreover, " for the present "—implying that more were to come. But the Houses went very much further. They gave this most solemn assurance : in " the war which is likely to ensue," "*we your loyal and loving subjects will never fail to assist your Majesty, in a parliamentary way.*" So not only would more be forthcoming but subsidies *more to the purpose*. But Gardiner is silent on that. Let the reader note well these few words. *They are plain, unconditional, absolute; provided there be*

---

[10] *History of England* (1908), V, p. 201.
[11] This section is omitted by Prothero, a few dots inserted instead ; see *Select Statutes,* p. 318.

" a real war," supplies without fail shall be voted. And therein we see the King's case. Who, indeed, could in honour deny it? And mark " in a parliamentary way "—not by this or that specified method as, for instance, the voting of subsidies—nothing ruled out *a priori.* Of that, again, Gardiner says nothing. The words had been taken, I think, from the King's speech on March the 14th. May not Williams have had them in mind in referring to alternative measures in his speech the next year at Westminster? [12]

The mention among " the four points " of " others your Majesty's friends and allies " is by no means, I think, incidental. They are, indeed, emphasized later; their prosperity is " deeply engaged "; the whole document ends on that note. Gardiner makes passing allusion to " the vague clause about assisting ' other your Majesty's friends and allies.' " [13] It was bound in a sense to be vague, for the King must look round for his friends, and not all could at that time be named. If, moreover, we turn for a moment to the speech that James made to the Houses on Sunday, the 14th of March, this particular phrase will be seen to acquire even greater importance than that which I just now assigned it. " But, my Lords and Gentlemen all, ye must give me leave, on the other side, to consider the possibility of the action; for in this case I must do as a man that makes a fortification, which must have outworks and inworks; so I must not deal only with my own people, but with my neighbours and allies, to assist me in so great a business as the recovery of the Palatinate. And, in this case, it is not sufficient to have the hearts of my subjects, without the help of my neighbours and allies; and, except particular means be set down, it will neither be a bridle to the adversaries of that cause, nor a comfort to my friends, who will join with me : general words will not carry it; therefore I must resort to particular means, and follow the counsel of our Saviour Christ in the Gospel; before I begin a war, to see how I can maintain it, as I told

---

[12] See p. 20, *supra.*
[13] *History of England,* V, p. 202.

you in my former answer." [14] This was frank and incisive enough. He must "deal with his neighbours and allies." Before he engages in war he must see his way clear to maintain it. Then the Houses adopt the King's attitude—even the King's phraseology—in drafting the address we have quoted. Moreover, on the 8th of the month he impressed other points on the Houses: "By sending of ambassadors; by maintenance of my children, and by assisting of the Palatinate, I have incurred a great debt to the King of Denmark, which I am not yet able to pay. The Low Countries, who, in regard of their nearness, are fittest to help for the recovery of the Palatinate, are at so low an ebb, that, if I assist them not, they are scarce able to subsist. The princes of Germany, that should do me any good, are all poor, wrecked, and disheartened, and do expect assistance from hence." [15] Here, I think, we can see why it was that the Houses on March the 23rd more particularly referred in their paper to "the States of the United Provinces." Their position in Europe would render them "fittest," as James says, "to help." But Christian and the princes of Germany were also among the King's allies, and money was needed to help them. The Commons were left in no doubt of the nature and scope of his policy, and that, too, before they had promised their own unconditional aid. He, moreover, had time after time made it perfectly clear that his aim was throughout to restore the Palatinate. However, we find Gardiner writing as though all these things never happened. To take but a single example, he says of Coke's speech in July: "The whole display of military preparation flashed thus suddenly before their eyes, created astonishment rather than any other feeling." [16]

A word upon Gardiner's remarks on the subsidies voted to James. "Evidently, therefore," says he, "neither party was in any way bound to anything beyond the expenditure of the 300,000l. already offered. When the next session began

[14] *Lords' Journals*, III, p. 265, March 17, 1624; Rushworth, p. 136.
[15] *L.J.*, III, p. 250; Rushworth, p. 130.
[16] *History*, V, p. 372.

it would be open to the King to say, if he thought fit, that he had found the enterprise more arduous than he had expected; and it would be equally open to the Commons to say that they declined to support any particular policy which the Crown had resolved to adopt." [17] " If you shall be engaged in a real war, we your loyal and loving subjects will never fail to assist your Majesty, in a parliamentary way." That phrase in itself should suffice. But, apart from that statement entirely, we find a direct refutation in James's plain words to the Houses that " undertaking the war, I must go through with it one way or other, though I should sell jewels and all." [18] These words also Gardiner ignores. If the King thus in March " must go through with it," how could he hold himself open to come in the autumn to parliament, pleading he found it too arduous and so, I suppose, must abandon it?

Gardiner contends that the King " had already promised [that is, on March the 14th] to call Parliament together for purposes of domestic legislation. He now promised to give an account at the same time of the expenditure already agreed on, and to ask the sanction of the Houses to the further prosecution of the war." [19] James promised on March the 14th not to make any treaty of peace without seeking their special advice : " I will never enter into any agreement, or treaty of composition, for satisfaction or peace, which is the end of war (else it is unjust and unchristian), without your advice." [20] And, again, upon March 23 : " In my last speech, I promised, that, if I accepted your offer, I would follow your advice, and would not after hearken to any treaty of peace, without first acquainting you, and requiring your advice." [21] This, I think, is not mentioned by Gardiner. Indeed, it goes ill with the notion that James was to ask for their sanction to continue the war in the autumn, and that in turn goes very ill with the King's unequivocal statement that " undertaking the war, I must go through with it one way or

[17] *Ibid.*, V, p. 202.
[18] *L.J.*, III, p. 283.
[19] *History*, V, p. 202.
[20] *L.J.*, III, p. 266.
[21] *Ibid.*, III, p. 283.

other." James's answers are turned into nonsense by the meaning that Gardiner puts on them. And, while he would not end the war without asking the Houses of Parliament, I find no foundation whatever for Gardiner's so positive statement that he " promised " " to ask the sanction of the Houses to the further prosecution of the war." True, he said upon March 23 : " In the next session, you will consider how this hath been husbanded ; and, according to that, think what is next to be done; and it will spur you the more to enable me for the rest, whereof I spake to you before." But this surely refers to supply? " You will consider how this [grant] hath been husbanded and, according to that [the way it hath been husbanded], think what is next to be done [that is, by you, in the way of supply]." The words are " what is next to be done " and " enable [finance] me for the rest " ; they are not " whether more shall be done," which or something like which we should need, if continuing the war were intended. Nor can " what is next to be done " have applied to the conduct of war. James declared they must leave that to him. " Whether I shall send twenty thousand or ten thousand, whether by sea or by land, East or West, by diversion or otherwise, by invasion upon the Bavarian or the Emperor, you must leave that to the King." [22] Gardiner seems very hard pressed ; he is driven to remark of this statement that " James, in talking of sending twenty thousand men or ten thousand men, was clearly not referring to anything connected with the present vote, but to the use to be made of the further subsidies which he expected in the autumn." [23] This statement the context refutes. For the words that precede are as follows : " But I desire you to understand, I must have a faithful and secret council of war, that must not be ordered by a multitude, for so my designs might be discovered beforehand. A penny of this money shall not be bestowed, but in the sight of your own committees." [24] Clearly it is to *this*

[22] *L.J.*, III, p. 283 ; Rushworth, p. 138. Rushworth has somewhat absurdly " But whether I shall send twenty thousand pounds or ten thousand pounds."
[23] *History*, V, p. 202.
[24] *L.J.*, III, p. 283.

money, the subsidies already voted, not future hypothetical subsidies, that the King's statement alludes.

One word of the autumn session. We are told, as we saw, that the King " had already promised to call Parliament together for purposes of domestic legislation." The King did not use the word " promise " ; he used " resolution " instead ; " my resolution is, to make this a session, with the passing of as many good laws as in convenient time may be prepared ; and at Michaelmas, or within few days after, to have a new session, and another in the spring." [25] The Houses did not meet in the autumn—a fact some, perhaps, may regret.[26] It would still remain true, notwithstanding, that, even if James's " resolution " were construed to mean " pledge " or " promise," *their* pledges did not depend on it.

There are two further pleas for the Commons. The first amounts briefly to this. Past engagements, indeed, are admitted ; but the Commons could not have been bound, it is argued, by a previous parliament.[27] The answer is twofold, I think. No such view of the matter, it seems, was adopted by the Commons themselves. Nor did James himself thus understand them. " We your loyal and loving subjects will never fail to assist your Majesty, in a parliamentary way." They spoke for the nation at large, and, moreover, they spoke " for the future." Such addresses as this, we repeat, cannot come very short of petitions or even of bills in their force. If, again, through the death of a sovereign, engagements were not to be binding, no war could be well undertaken. The Crown could not know where it stood for so much as a few weeks together. Not so could a war be conducted or policies

[25] *Ibid.*, III, p. 266 ; Rushworth, p. 138. See Gardiner in the *Fawsley Debates,* " The King's promise to summon Parliament in the autumn was no less broken " (p. iv.).

[26] The reason assigned then was sickness ; Chamberlain to Carleton, October 9, in *State Papers Domestic, 1623–5,* p. 352. Chamberlain reported to Carleton three or four hundred deaths to the week (October 23 ; *ibid.*, p. 350). Coke to Brooke on October 1 : " The new sickness continueth both in city and country. This week there died 411 " (*Coke MSS.*, I, p. 172).

[27] Wentworth thus argued at Oxford : " The engagement of a former parliament bindeth not this " (*Commons' Journals,* I, p. 814, August 10). Incidentally, this, of course, proves the engagements themselves not in doubt.

framed and adjusted. The principle with which I am dealing, that the House could not bind its successor, would have led to conclusions which the Commons themselves had been first to reject. There were ever two parties, two sides in those times in all public transactions. It follows that with each dissolution the King's own engagements would end. And both sides must adhere to a bargain or both be together released.

The second plea seems to be this. The Commons in 1624 wanted war with the Spaniards at sea; they did not want a war upon land, which was James's idea, so we gather, and much less a war upon both, which, it seems, was in Buckingham's mind. There were three different schemes in the air, and the Commons were opposed to the King on a serious question of policy.[28] This plea, I suppose, comes to saying that the Commons were thinking very little, if at all, of recovering the Palatinate. Gardiner, for instance, remarks of the lengthy debate on supply in the Commons on March the 19th: "On the prospect opened to them of a Continental war they were more outspoken. Sir Francis Seymour touched the question to the quick. He had heard 'wars spoken on,' he said, 'and an army; but would be glad to hear where. The Palatinate was the place intended by his Majesty. This we never thought of, nor is it fit for the consideration of the House in regard of the infinite charge.' Not a word was uttered in opposition to the view thus taken by Seymour. The House was looking in another direction than the Palatinate. 'Are we poor?' cried Eliot, 'Spain is rich. There are our Indies. Break with them; we shall break our necessities together!' "[29] I do not well see how this plea can survive a few moments' inspection. Suppose that the facts were as stated. But James on all possible occasions had made it as plain as could be that he had but one object throughout—to recover or restore the Palatinate. The Commons knew this very well, when they drafted their famous address. If they had a different object from James and a

---

[28] See Gardiner, for instance, on the Commons in his *History*, V, pp. 190ff.

[29] *Ibid.*, V, p. 199.

different, even opposite policy, the last thing they ought to have done was to pledge their unconditional aid. Such a pledge was not only misleading but also entirely uncalled for. I fail to see any excuse for their thus going out of their way, and, if misunderstandings resulted, the blame must rest wholly upon them. They adopted, moreover, and approved James's scheme of Continental alliances—"the assistance of your neighbours, the States of the United Provinces, and others your Majesty's friends and allies." [30] We are asked to believe that the Commons were opposed to a Continental war. They had heard all that James had to tell them of Germany, Denmark and elsewhere, and yet they went out of their way to refer to those " neighbours and allies " as fit to receive such assistance. And no one could say that " assistance " precluded the sending of troops. If they did not agree with the King, they had merely to leave the phrase out. And, if misunderstandings resulted, we must, upon any such view, hold them once more entirely to blame. They cannot be excused on the ground of not wanting a quarrel with James. They created their own difficulties—went out of their way to create them. While James's position was plain, theirs, to say the very least, was ambiguous, if not of set purpose double-tongued.

SUPPLY AND " SOME ART "

We have seen how Charles viewed the position and what were the Commons' engagements, their solemn protestations and pledges. How, then, did they answer his plea, when at length they proceeded to business, on Tuesday, the 21st June ? They had no sooner met than a motion by Mallory, member for Ripon, supported by Phelips and Wentworth, was made for adjournment till Michaelmas. [31] Such motions, however,

---

[30] Mark, too, the following words :—" Your kingdom (the weal and safety whereof is, in our judgements, apparently threatened, if . . . that provision for the defence of your realm, and aid of your friends and allies, be not reasonably made)."

[31] *Fawsley Debates,* p. 7 ; *Commons' Journals,* I, p. 800. Forster's reference to " the *Journals* (I, p. 799) " is inaccurate, and the words that he quotes from Phelips, " to other time and place," should read " to some other time or place." See *Sir John Eliot,* I, p. 241, footnote.

were " rare," as, indeed, Phelips slyly allowed. When did
parliament last move the Crown that it thus be so sharply
" put off " ? Let supplies, in effect, be refused and their own
solemn pledges disowned; let the King be debarred from
explaining his needs, preparations, engagements. The House
for the most part recoiled from inflicting so crude a rebuff
and thus damning their address to King James as a shred of
false parchment outright. Even Phelips harangued them in
vain. There were methods as honest, more subtle. Go into
committee, said Alford, and settle what line should be taken—
a course, to say least, more respectful.[32] And Heath, the
Solicitor-General, who led at that time for the Crown,
followed suit with much judgement and tact. Let the House,
he said, name a committee to consider the needs of the
moment—in substance, the motion by Alford.[33] The motion
for adjournment was shelved, as a motion for moving from
London—" suppressed," say the records, " by order." [34] Next
day the debate was continued, a Committee of Grievances
moved for,[35] and Alford repeated his motion.[36] No grievances,
said Sir E. Coke, since the new king ascended the throne.[37]
Not a word about tonnage and poundage, on which they were
later to harp. So the talk for a time roamed at large, and all
manners of motions cropped up, to consider which on the next
morning the House would go into committee.[38] And so in the
upshot we find that all points of " supply and religion "
" stood committed to the whole House "—otherwise, " to the
Great Committee," " Mr. Speaker sitting by "—" wherein "
(let these words be well noted) " religion was to have the first
place." [39] Till " religion " was out of the way they would not
hear a word of " supply," though supply must have been on
their conscience.

For a week, then, " religion " " preceded." They had

[32] *Commons' Journals,* I, p. 800.
[33] *Fawsley Debates,* p. 8.
[34] *Ibid.,* p. 8.
[35] *Commons' Journals,* I, p. 800 ; *Fawsley Debates,* p. 9.
[36] *Commons' Journals,* I, p. 800.
[37] *Fawsley Debates,* p. 12.
[38] *Commons' Journals,* I, p. 801.
[39] *Fawsley Debates,* p. 16.

previously asked for " a fast," which the King very graciously granted, and brought a bill into the House against breaking the Sunday or "Sabbath"—a sin, we presume, far more heinous than breaking one's most solemn pledges.   Much time was now spent upon drafting a so-called "petition of religion."   Not only would Pym ban the Papists; he would have banned all but the Calvinists.   Charles and the bishops by contrast stood then for a relative freedom.   Let us lightly pass over such matters; they have much of interest, doubtless, but led to no breach with the Crown and, as such, are of minor importance.   This zeal for religion, however, as cloaking more subtle designs, is essential to clear understanding.   At length on the last day of June their petition was well under way and " religion " thus safely disposed of.[40]   "The Country" were there in full force.   For the most part, however, "the courtiers" were not to be found in their places, not expecting some subtle diversion.[41]   Secretary Morton himself was away on a mission in Holland and could hardly be back for some weeks.   Then it was that without more ado Seymour moved to go into supply and concluded by proposing a grant of one subsidy, one fifteenth—little short of a total refusal.[42]   No more should Charles have for the war, not to mention his father's funeral, his own coronation and so on.   The Court were no match for such tactics.   And no one spoke up for the King save the fluent and versatile Rudyerd, who made the best case that he could but had clearly received no instructions and asked for no definite sum.   For Sir Benjamin the King was a prince well-disposed to and bred among parliaments.   Discussion, it seems, was protracted.[43]   Opinion at first was divided, and some were for more, some for less.   Two subsidies, most of them said.   But the sense of the House was apparent, when Phelips got up to take part and declared for two subsidies only.   Sandys,

[40] *Ibid.*, p. 30.
[41] " Who were most of them absent in the beginning of this motion, as not expecting this would have fallen out a day for that business " (*Fawsley Debates*, p. 33).
[42] For this very important sitting see *Fawsley Debates,* pp. 30-3.   The *Journals* contain a blank from the 22nd of June to the 4th of July.
[43] " Debate wavered a good while " (*Fawsley Debates,* p. 30).

D

Wentworth, Sir E. Coke went with him, as though they were acting together. The issue, in short, was decided, when some of the King's men came in, unaware of the course of debate, though " provided to have spoken," we are told in the chronicler's very quaint English, " and meant to have urged for a larger proportion." These were the men with instructions to argue the case for the Crown. But no whips kept a house for the King; and no King's men could now turn the tide, and the vote was a foregone conclusion. Intervention, remonstrance seemed useless. What else could they do but keep silent? [44] Then Phelips's motion went through. Charles was not to be heard by the Commons; his case was to go by default. A surprise had been sprung on the Court, and " some art " had been used to the purpose. A snap vote, in fact, had been taken, to put it in plain, modern jargon. Having promised their utmost assistance, they whittled it down to a minimum, leaving the King in the lurch, and proved false to their most solemn pledges, whereby—indeed, whereby alone—they had brought the Crown into a war. They, moreover, now had it both ways; they were free, as before, to criticize and discredit the conduct of the war. We must give them, however unscrupulous, the credit (for what it is worth) of devising a most subtle tactic.

THE CUSTOMS OR TONNAGE AND POUNDAGE

What was the King now to do? To abandon the policy the Commons so vigorously pressed on his father without fresh entreaty or effort? " Whereunto you have betrayed me "— how true a presentiment, surely! A subsidy roughly amounted in pounds to a mere seventy thousand. And the King needed more like a million. Customs and subsidies together would not cover even a third. Thus the vote appeared trifling, derisory. If bitter with disappointment, if sore and resentful at heart from a treatment so false and unseemly, the King at least kept his good temper. While

---

[44] " So, though divers were provided to have spoken and meant to have urged for a larger proportion, yet not knowing how the debate had passed, and seeing no likelihood of prevailing, they held their peace " (*Fawsley Debates*, p. 33).

declining to hasten their proceedings, he offered on July the 4th, when the Houses declared themselves ready, to end this unfortunate session. Since the plague grew apace in the city, he would take the more care of their health, and as Phelips and others at first were desirous of being " put off," you would think they would welcome this offer.

But the Commons had more work to do. In spite of the promised adjournment, the House had by no means " grown thin " ; two hundred and twenty odd members were soon to take part in the vote upon Wentworth's election for Yorkshire. Their leaders were now in no haste and were busy with Montague's books, thus resuming the cloak of religion.   One triumph suggested another.   The Tonnage and Poundage Bill was brought in on the 5th of July and a second time read the same day.[45]   The grant was, as usual, for life in the bill as brought into the House and drawn up by the leading Crown lawyers. And so it was " time out of mind."   The customs had gone with the Crown since the days of King Edward the Fourth ; without them no kingdom, no king. Their continued and formal renewal had created Crown property in them ; and until they were formally voted, the Crown had enforced their collection.   But Phelips and Seymour and others now moved for a strict limitation, " to our Lady Day next," " for a year."   Moreover, the duties on cloths, books of rates, impositions and what not must all, so they claimed, be gone into before they had done with the matter.   Heath endeavoured to meet them half-way.   On the King's legal rights he was silent.   He could have appealed to the case of John Bates in the Court of Exchequer. Instead he appealed to tradition, " so many descents," as he called them.   Apart from the Court of Exchequer, all the " rights " that there were in the matter, the Crown's and the Commons' alike, rested wholly on nothing but custom. While, therefore, against limitations, he " yielded " that the bill be committed and moved that a clause be inserted for saving the " rights " of the Commons in regard to those

---

[45] See for this debate *Commons' Journals,* I, p. 803 ; *Fawsley Debates,* p. 43.

matters put forward as grounds for a temporary grant.[46] If
the object was simply to deal with the difficulties pleaded by
members and save certain " rights " of the House, then the
course Heath proposed was the right one. The fact of its
being rejected must prove those pleas nothing but pretexts.
The case that was made for the Commons the Crown was
prepared to concede. What cause for complaint then
remained? For the new reign commenced with *concession*
in spite of the 30th June. Should there not now have been
a concordat, a swift and most happy agreement, preserving
the " rights " on both sides and, as such, to both sides satisfy-
ing? But Phelips and Seymour insisted; the scheme, we are
told, was their " darling." [47] The grant was for one year
alone in the bill as it came from Committee, and, in spite of
some words that were used, we may fairly suppose them
unwilling to grant in the future for life. They refused, in
effect, to compromise; they were bent at all costs on their
ends. So this day and the last day of June marked the first
great assaults on the Crown. Charles could neither make war
without subsidies nor live without tonnage and poundage.
They refused him the means to make war; he should have
no assured means of living, so far as that lay in their power.
For it needed no special prevision, so great were, indeed, his
embarrassments, to see that his household would starve, if
deprived of the tonnage and poundage—a point we shall
shortly return to in dealing with his empty exchequer—and,
in truth, this grim fact may by now very well have become
common knowledge. They would starve the King into submission. To strike, in a word, at the customs, was to strike
at the roots of the monarchy. Red revolution, in short, was
now looming upon the horizon.

TONNAGE AND POUNDAGE IN THE LORDS

The Bill for the Tonnage and Poundage was read a third
time in the Commons, it seems, upon July the 8th,[48] and the

---

[46] *Fawsley Debates,* p. 44 ; " yet he yielded it should be committed, and
that some short proviso might be annexed to save our right in those
questions."

[47] *Scrinia Reserata,* II, p. 17 ; see also p. 38, *infra.*

[48] *Commons' Journals,* I, p. 807.

grant was for one year alone.[49] It was sent to the Lords on
the 9th and was read a first time the same day.[50] The *Lords'
Journals* have no further entry, and no further progress was
made with it. We may with some reason infer that the bill
was distasteful to the Lords and was, therefore, in plain
language, dropped. They may well have seen through the
design; but they counted in those days for little and possibly
fought somewhat shy of inviting a quarrel with the Commons.
It is otherwise hard to conjecture, in view of the approaching
adjournment, why it was not at once passed. It would seem
that the Commons expected it. " It was agreed to be the
custom that we ought to send for the Bill of subsidies by the
laity, and the Speaker to carry it up. Concerning the Bill for
the other subsidies of Tonnage and Poundage there were a
question made; but it was not resolved, because the House
was informed that that Bill was not passed." [51] Yet the Lords
were apparently idle, and Eliot himself so describes them—
" having dealt in little at this meeting, and having no
business at that time." [52] Moreover, on July the 5th, in reply
to a message from the Commons, the Lords " did promise
expedition of the Bills sent, and to be sent, unto their Lord-
ships," [53] but denied it as soon as the 9th to a bill of so vast
an importance and, indeed, made no progress at all with it,
when they reassembled at Oxford. Parliament was adjourned,
not prorogued; so the bill, like the Recusants Bill, could have
been carried forward in August. How very unlike the prompt
treatment accorded to the Subsidies Bill, which passed the

[49] The *precise* limitation seems uncertain and also, I think, immaterial.
Says the writer of the *Fawsley Debates*: " This grant related to the 27
of March 1625 [the date of the King's accession] and was to continue
until the 27 of March 1626 " (p. 47). But Mallett on August the 9th
said " till 25 Martii next," if the *Journals* for that date are right.
[50] *Commons' Journals*, I, p. 807; *Lords' Journals*, III, pp. 462–3. The
list of " Bills brought in this Session " has also the following entry: " 1ª
vice lecta 9 Julii 1625. An Act of a Subsidy of Tonnage and Poundage "
(*Lords' Journals*, III, p. 490).
[51] *Fawsley Debates*, p. 66.
[52] *Negotium Posterorum* (ed. Grosart), I, p. 119. That the Lords had
but little to do is borne out by two letters from Mandeville. See
Buccleugh MSS., I, pp. 260, 261.
[53] *Lords' Journals*, III, p. 456.

same day through all stages![54]   But the Lords must have
known that the customs would continue to be levied by
Charles, as in previous reigns, prior to granting.

That Williams, who still was Lord Keeper and, therefore,
a servant of Charles, had a hand of some sort in the matter,
though whether at London or Oxford we cannot unfortunately say, must, I think, be considered as certain.   In a paper
he gave to the King on the following 14th of August,
" Reasons to satisfy your most excellent Majesty concerning
my carriage all this last Parliament," the Keeper took credit
to himself for " crossing the popular way, more than any of
the Council; which I durst not have done, if I had intended
to run along with them . . . 4.   In direct opposition to the
Lord Saye, in staying the Bill of Tonnage and Poundage,
which was the darling of the active part in the House of
Commons."   Williams could not have said that in a statement
intended for Charles, if it had no foundation in fact, and
it seems to me very unlikely he took his instructions from
Charles.   He was playing, I think, his own game.   But no
peer could have " stayed " the Lords' House, had they wished
to proceed with a bill.[55]   Notwithstanding, that the bill was
" the darling " of Seymour and Phelips and others is a statement of vital importance.   It clearly discloses their hand, and
it follows that their zeal for " religion " and assigning it a
certain priority were means to confusing the issue and thus,
as we said, hypocritical.

And here let me bring up a question which I cannot
entirely resolve.   The reports of the 5th of July have the
following very strange entries.   " Sir Edw. Coke :—Disliketh
the word, ' advice of the Lords ' " ;   so much and no more
say the *Journals*.[56]   " Sir Ed[ward] Cooke excepted against
these words, advised by the Lords. 9. H. [Henry] 4, the
Lords moved for a subsidy, which the Commons would not
endure " ;   so the *Fawsley Debates*.[57]   Both these entries

[54] *Lords' Journals*, III, p. 461.
[55] *Scrinia Reserata*, II, p. 17.   He also took credit for " lingering and
staying the Bill against Recusants."   Williams was then out of favour
and soon to be dismissed by the King.
[56] I, p. 803.
[57] p. 44.

immediately follow the speech made by Heath for the Crown;
we are, therefore, inclined to conjecture that the words to
which Coke took exception had fallen from Heath in debate.
They point to some sort of intervention on the part of the
Lords in the case, though I find no allusion in their *Journals*.
Did they prompt in one way or another the proposal Heath
made in the Commons and " move," as it were, " for a
subsidy "?   If something of this kind had happened, we
should, I think, comprehend better the fate of the bill in their
House.   If, however, my suggestion is rejected, the entries
still need explanation, and this may prove no easy matter.[58]
One fact, at least, plainly emerges.   For none, as we said,
could imagine that the customs could go uncollected.   With
levying without act of parliament the King could thus later
be charged, as indeed, he was very soon after,[59] and motives
in matters of policy are aften disclosed by effects.   Was it
Williams's unavowed object to bring about such a result?
He was shrewd enough, at least, to foresee it and humbug
enough to promote it.

AN EMPTY EXCHEQUER

This brings us without more ado to the state of the Crown
revenues when the young King ascended the throne.   Great,
indeed, must have been his embarrassments.   Let us recite
some plain facts.   Thus we read of an empty exchequer as
early as June the 11th in a letter to Conway from Ley.[60]   A
month later Locke, writing to Carleton, was telling the same
sorry story: " My last to your lordship was of the 30. of
June ; I have since spoken to my Lo. Tre'r and to Sir Robert
Pye about your Lordship's moneys, but for the present can
give your Lordship small hope of receiving them, the want of
moneys being so great as the like hath not been known.   Sir
Edward Barrett and Mr. Rawlins stay of purpose for want of

---

[58] On this phrase, the " advice of the Lords," some remarks that
Lord Clarendon makes of a seemingly similar incident may, I think, well
be compared *(History,* I, pp. 189–90).

[59] By Phelips on August the 5th, though the Houses were actually
sitting and parliament not yet dissolved. See *Fawsley Debates,* p. 81.

[60] *State Papers, Domestic Series,* 1625–6, p. 41.

money, and since midsummer neither bedchamber man, nor pensioner, nor any other servant of the King, hath received any penny. All the money that is yet in the Exchequer will not serve to feed the French; the Duchess of Chevreux being now resolved to lie in here, for which purpose beer, wine, and other provisions are laid in at Richmond." [61] Burlamachi was begging of Conway " that his 20,000*l*. may be borne in mind. If he does not receive some part of it, it will be his ruin." [62] Burlamachi was a foreign money-lender, the Rothschild, it seems, of the day. A week later we read the same story—" no money now in the Exchequer." [63] Sir Robert Karr, writing to Conway, reported about the same date : " There is not so much in the Privy Purse as will give the nurse of Madame Chevreuse and the midwife that which must be done for the King's honour." [64] Then May told the Commons in August : " If the King's plate or jewels, or the plate and jewels of some others, whom he hears dashed upon, could have procured money, we had not met here now." [65] Ley, moreover, informed both the Houses that Charles " hath anticipated upon the customs and revenue to be due for the year ensuing the sum of 200,000 pounds, so as we are in question how to maintain him with bread and meat." [66] Thus the customs or the tonnage and poundage had been taken already in advance and devoted, whether partly or wholly, to keeping his household alive. Such, indeed, were the straits of the King that he hardly knew how to get food. He was ready to pawn the Crown Jewels.[67] So had James been prepared, as we saw.[68] Then the King himself borrowed large sums with a view to financing the war. He had borrowed, moreover, as Prince and came burdened with

[61] *Fawsley Debates*, p. 152 ; *S.P.D.*, p. 57. Barrett was " Ambassador for France," Rawlins " Agent at the Court of Savoy " (*Coke MSS.*, I, p. 192 ; *S.P.D.*, p. 535). Yet they could not proceed to their posts !

[62] *S.P.D.*, p. 60.

[63] *Ibid.*, p. 67 (Lord Treasurer Ley to Secretary Conway).

[64] *Ibid.*, p. 73. Chevreuse had come with the Queen.

[65] *Fawsley Debates*, p. 78.

[66] *Ibid.*, p. 104. Gardiner mentions this fact without comment (V, p. 403).

[67] The State Papers have numerous allusions.

[68] See p. 27, *supra*.

debt to the throne.[69]   For so strong was his faith in the
Commons, who had pledged themselves up to the hilt.   It was
part of this money just mentioned that Philip Burlamachi
alluded to.   James had been deeply in debt and had even
suggested a grant of one subsidy, two fifteens, " yearly, until
my debts be paid."   This request was, however, withdrawn.[70]
Charles inherited James's engagements ; he inherited also his
debts.

To return now to tonnage and poundage, we repeat that the
Commons intended to starve the King into submission and
leave him without " bread and meat " or accuse him of
collecting the customs without any grant by the Commons.
They thus had two strings to their bow.   And once more we
may certainly grant them the credit (for what it is worth)
of devising a most subtle tactic, unscrupulous, reckless and
anarchic.

Ley's statement in the following year I suppose to bear
out our contention.   He wrote that the tonnage and poundage
" was assigned in part for the King's Household, and the
remainder for certain sea services.   If such assignment were
broken, the House must of necessity break." [71]

Among modern historians, Mr. Fletcher, in spite of belittling
the King, has the grace to admit the main point, when
in passing he says that " the King, who simply couldn't
live at all without this resource, collected the customs, without
any grant, right down to 1640." [72]   Thus he might have been
expected to see that the strategy of Charles's opponents was
based in the main on this fact.   So, again, in deprecating their
resort to a measure admittedly " violent," he supposes no
need for such measures with " such a stupid king " as was
Charles, when he might have more reasonably inferred that
the House took a far different measure of the young King's
capacities and qualities and also in that sense a juster.
Mr. Fletcher, indeed, goes so far as to make the very curious

[69] See *Fawsley Debates*, p. 103.
[70] See, for example, *Lords' Journals*, III, p. 266.
[71] *S.P.D.*, p. 314.
[72] *An Introductory History of England from Henry VII to the
Restoration*, p. 281.

statement that the Commons " acknowledged their error " by making at first small complaint of the King for collecting the dues. No complaint of the kind was legitimate. Phelips was complaining in August. And the Commons were still at this game (see our preface) some sixteen years later.

ACCOUNTS AND ESTIMATES

And now to return to the Commons, who were, as we saw, in no hurry. Coke rose in his place on the 8th and delivered a message from the King [73]—in the words of the *Fawsley Debates,* " to give the House true information of his Majesty's estate, as he doubts not that we came together with true affections." Sir John was a Master of Requests, conscientious, methodical, able, and soon to hold Morton's great office. By this time he also directed all matters concerning the navy. He spoke of the subsidies first, for " his Majesty," so he informed them, " graciously accepts the gift which is already resolved of, as a welcome and pledge of the love not only of this representative body, but of the whole kingdom : yet he takes notice of our anticipation of that business, and that we fell into it without intervention of any ministers of state, which he imputes to our forwardness in his service, and confidence in his favour and correspondency with us." The King, he then went on to say, " is very well satisfied in our care and diligence to examine the account " (which, among others, Phelips had asked for),[74] " not doubting but we shall find that not a penny of it hath come into the Exchequer, or diverted to any other uses but such as were intended." Coke stated the various expenses—" particular disbursements " he called them. Describing how James himself treated with this or that party or prince, he replied to complaints and criticisms directed against the royal policy, dealing at length with Count Mansfeld. He turned to the estimates next, for " his Majesty rests not here, but hath commanded to give you an

[73] " Reporteth a commandment from his Majesty " ; " Message from the King " in the margin *(Commons' Journals,* I, p. 806) ; " by commandment from the King " *(Fawsley Debates,* p. 56) ; " by his Majesty's command," Locke to Carleton *(F.D.,* p. 153).

[74] On June 21 and June 30 ; see *Fawsley Debates,* pp. 7, 31.

account of that which is and will be spent upon the preparation now in hand." Then each item was duly set out, not a
fact nor a figure kept back. Some at least of " the businesses "
mentioned required " farther help " from the Commons or
else what he called " some new way," " the ordinary revenue
being exhausted and overcharged with other expenses both of
necessity and honour." Before he ascended the throne,
Charles himself borrowed twenty thousand pounds, while the
Duke and some other Court officers found over ninety-four
thousand.[75] Coke urged they should not be " undone " by
their being so ready to help. Would the House so " proclaim
its own poverty "? Moreover, the fleet must go forth, for
upon it all else now depended. However, he declared it
" impossible for these things to subsist but by money or credit.
A present resolution for money is not expected. It remains
we should give thanks to his Majesty for his care of us by
engaging himself so deeply, and whereof he thought fit we
should go truly informed into our countries, that so we may
the better satisfy the people, and in the meantime it is
requisite we should express our own affection to the business
now in hand, and that when we return again we are willing
to relieve his Majesty in some farther proportion : and
whether this be fit to be kept within the walls of the House,
and not by some public message to the King, or other
signification, to declare our forwardness to supply the actions
now begun, he humbly left to the wisdom of the House "—
a modest proposal, when viewed in the light of that famous
address !

But the motion was coldly received and was seconded only
by Beecher, then one of the Clerks of the Council. Giles and
Littleton both spoke adversely. The members were most of
them sullen. On either side little was said. So apparent,
indeed, was their temper, that Heath " laid aside " Coke's
suggestion and put the best face on the matter. In the
subsidies and tonnage and poundage they " sufficiently
expressed their affections." Let none ever speak in that

[75] No better proof could be found that the King had his heart in the
business and that there was thus " a real war."

House but as though Spanish Philip could hear him. But let them at least, on returning, " bring with them the hearts of true Englishmen." [76] Coke, notwithstanding, himself three days later repeated his motion, to judge by this very brief entry, " that his proposition was, should declare ourselves, we would not now leave him in it." I find nothing more on the records.[77]

For the motives that prompted the message the King sent by Coke to the Commons we need, I think, hardly look far. For, to use Coke's polite but apt phrase, they had " anticipated the business " by what we now call a snap vote. But the King had undertaken to explain both his own and his father's engagements and promised a statement of accounts. He would keep his pledged word to the Commons in spite of parliamentary manoeuvres. The Commons should have facts and figures, should know all there was to be known. No money, however, should be asked for, no " motion of supply " be proposed. Coke's suggestion was open, I think, to one plausible criticism only. The House had grown empty by now. Was he not taking undue advantage and springing a motion upon them, how vague in its language soever, in the hope that the few then remaining would commit all the others in absence? This objection rests on the assumption that Charles knew the House was grown thin. But that prior to the 8th he knew this we have no means whatever of proving. He knew it the same afternoon; that is all we can now say for certain.[78] He well may have taken for granted that members were still there in force, inasmuch as no message had reached him in regard to the proffered adjournment. Moreover, his message of the 4th had in no way prevented

[76] *Fawsley Debates*, pp. 56–9; *Commons' Journals*, I, p. 806. The latter are practically useless, giving only some phrases of Coke's. Coke was seconded by others than Beecher, according to a letter from Locke, who, however, does not mention names, using only the vague phrase, " by some " (*Fawsley Debates*, p. 153). But the *Fawsley Debates* are explicit: " This motion was seconded by none but by Sir W[illia]m Beecher "—not a point upon which, one imagines, the writer could well be mistaken. He must have been present throughout, for he seems to make a note of the fact, when he chanced to be " out of the House."

[77] *Commons' Journals*, I, p. 808.

[78] See p. 69, n. 145, *infra*.

the Commons from proceeding to tonnage and poundage or proceeding with Montague's books. Of the latter they said on the 7th, in reply to a message from the Lords : " We are now in a serious and weighty business, which they [sic] conceive may hold long." [79] But, to waive any point of that nature, the objection with which I am dealing will be seen to lose all plausibility, once we recall to our minds the snap vote of the last day of June. Yet Phelips employed it at Oxford. He observed upon August the 5th : " The first resolution of our adjournment expressed in his Majesty's care of our health. But upon the Friday before our parting, a proposition was made by a gentleman [Coke], who did that yesterday which never any man did before. Did the House then think they did well? And shall we now vary? A surprise had then taken us, if God had not prevented it." [80] " An ambuscade and surprise," so did Eliot write as absurdly.[81] " Surprises " engineered by a Seymour were fair play to Phelips and Eliot ; the King's carrying out of his word, his attempt to retrieve the position, when a march had been stolen upon him, were condemned as " an ambuscade," from which providence only had saved them ! So providence, it seems, engineered in the persons of Seymour and others the snap vote that " took " the young King. As for binding the rest of the House, was not parliament already bound by the famous address to his father? Yet Charles still preserved his good temper and had no reply but a smile, when he heard on that same afternoon the full story of Montague's books.[82]

Some writers would seem to object to Coke's using the words, " some new way." " It was sure," of this phrase observes Gardiner, " to grate upon the ears of his hearers." [83] But what did Coke mean more precisely? We saw that on June the 18th the Lord Keeper was reported as stating that " if subsidies be thought too long and backward, his Majesty desires to hear, and not to propound, the manner thereof." [84]

[79] *Commons' Journals*, I, p. 805.
[80] *Fawsley Debates*, p. 80.
[81] See p. 76, *infra*.
[82] *Fawsley Debates*, p. 62.
[83] *History*, V, p. 371.
[84] See p. 20, *supra*.

" Subsidies," James had observed, " ask a great time to bring them in. Now, if you assist in that way, I must take them up beforehand upon credit, which will eat up a great part of them." [85]   Returning to the statement by Coke, we shall come upon this somewhat later : " It is impossible for these things to subsist but by money or credit." The same phrase recurs in the message that Coke himself brought to the House on the morning of July 11, " That the King hath given way to our recess ; but must of necessity call us together speedily again, for support of that war, wherein we have engaged him ; which cannot be done without money, or credit." [86]   There were, that is, only two ways, and by " credit " Coke meant, I think, " subsidies." If I am right in this surmise, " some new way " means what he calls " money " and " money " that alternative method Charles invited the House to put forward. In like manner, " money " and " credit " are once more opposed in a letter from Coke to Lord Brooke in the August : " But the resolution upon the present, which the King himself delivered to me in his chair was to show the importance of the fleet, and that it could not proceed without a present supply by money or credit." [87]   Some other method, indeed, was apparently talked of in London some time before parliament met. Thus a letter of May the 14th : " The parliament holds, but thought not above some twenty days, and that to settle the house, and devise some allowable and parliamentary way (though not in the nature of a subsidy for defect of coronation) to supply the present necessities of our warlike preparation. The judges, they say, sate about it ; but what they resolved the King I hear not. Yet some talk of a parliamentary contribution, if not in the full nature, yet in the name of a benevolence, which may be agreed upon without a session or royal assent, as not having the nature of a compulsive statute." [88]   These phrases, I suggest in conclusion, about " some new way " and so forth can be traced back to James's own statement : " Therefore, seeing you give me such fair

[85] *Lords' Journals,* III, p. 251 (March 8, 1624).
[86] *Commons' Journals,* I, p. 808.
[87] *Coke MSS.,* I, p. 208.
[88] Mead to Stuteville, *Court and Times of Charles the First,* I, p. 21.

general promises, I will deal freely with you, and tell you plainly what I think will do the turn; but whether it be by subsidies only, or other means that may be equivalent, is all one to me; for being done in parliament, is done by a parliamentary way." [89] That phrase, I may add, is itself a sufficient reply to those folk on whose ears " some new way " must have " grated."

Just one other point here in passing. " It remains," remarked Coke in his speech, " we should give thanks to his Majesty for his care of us by engaging himself so deeply, and whereof he thought fit we should go truly informed into our countries [counties], that so we may the better satisfy the people." The constituencies, therefore, Charles sought at this time to take into his confidence. Thus not the Commons alone, the electors he looked and appealed to—an attitude far from consistent with that of an arbitrary ruler. Indeed, he called more than one parliament, hoping for " better understandings," tolerating their subtlest intrigues, till his crown and his life seemed at stake.

PARLIAMENT ADJOURNED TO OXFORD

Coke had spoken on Friday, the 8th. On the following Monday, the 11th, Charles adjourned the two Houses to Oxford. A word or two here upon Gardiner, in whom we find these observations : " The Commons then proceeded to the Upper House to hear the Royal assent given to the few Bills which had been passed. The word 'shortly' was then explained to them by the Lord Keeper. There was to be an adjournment, not a prorogation. They were to meet again at Oxford on August 1." [90] " There was to be an adjournment, not a prorogation," as though it had been the King's choice or the Commons desired prorogation. But, unless I am greatly mistaken, the House itself chose an adjournment. We have seen the King's message by Williams,

---

[89] *Lords' Journals*, III, p. 266 ; Rushworth, p. 137.
[90] *History*, V, p. 373. " The few bills " were actually nine; they are specified in the *Lords' Journals* (III, 465). The " shortly " refers to the message by Coke on July the 11th; see *Commons' Journals*, I, p. 808 ; *Fawsley Debates*, p. 67.

delivered on July the 4th.[91]   That same day we find in the *Journals:* " Resolved, To agree upon a time, to be intimated to the King, for our recess; and for the manner of it; whether by adjournment, or with a session, and a bill, to continue all things in *statu quo*.   This to be done first to-morrow morning." [92]   To what was first done the next morning no reference is made in the *Journals*.[93]   That the Commons decided for adjournment seems plain from the following entry: " L. 1ª. L. 2ª.   An Act that this Session of Parliament shall not determine by his Majesty's Royal Assent to any Act or Acts of Parliament :—Committed to a Committee of the whole House :—This afternoon, after the subsidy done." [94]   This bill passed through all its stages on July the 8th in the Lords and received royal assent the next Monday.[95] Moreover, the date, in like manner, was apparently chosen by parliament.   This is implied in the message from Charles upon July the 4th.   Then we find that Strode moved on the 9th " to send to the King, for his licence to depart on Monday morning, according to his Majesty's intimation," and Heath, the Solicitor-General, " to desire a conference with the Lords, about the time of our recess.—Ordered."   " According to his Majesty's intimation " means " so soon as he shall understand of their readiness."   The Commons conveyed to the Lords at the conference suggested by Heath " our desire of recess upon Monday morning."   The Lord President " answered, our motion required no debate, but consent." [96]   Moreover, we have the King's answer delivered on July 11 :   " Sir Edw. Coke reporteth from the conference; that the Lord President delivered, that, as both Houses petitioned the King for a

[91] See p. 35, *supra;*   also appendix three, p. 174, *infra.*
[92] *Commons' Journals,* I, p. 803.
[93] Nor yet in the *Fawsley Debates.*
[94] *Commons' Journals,* I, p. 803 ;   *Fawsley Debates,* pp. 43, 55.   The report in the latter seems decisive: " Mr. Solicitor on the other part. That if we made it a session, the expectation of the country would be greater than if it were only an adjournment ;   and we shall have a more seasonable time thereafter to give them full satisfaction.   So the bill was past " (p. 55).   And the bill upon p. 43 is " an act for the adjournment of Parliament."
[95] *Lords' Journals,* III, pp. 461, 465.
[96] *Commons' Journals,* I, pp. 807, 808 ;   *Fawsley Debates,* p. 63.

recess this day, so his Majesty, respecting the paucity of the members of this House, and the danger of the sickness, is pleased, we shall recede this day: the particulars whereof we shall presently receive from the Lord Keeper's mouth." [97]

I may add that Locke wrote in a letter to Carleton on July the 9th: "The Parliament is like to break up upon Monday next: the King left it free to the House by his pleasure signified by Mr. Solicitor, to continue or dissolve as they should think fittest, having regard to the danger of the time and necessity of the State, promising to consent to the time that they should set down, which the House took as a gracious favour from his Majesty." [98] I cannot find anywhere else such a message by Mr. Solicitor. Locke gives no date in his letter. But the context appears to make clear it was prior to Coke's speech on the 8th. Locke, however, if wrong in the name, could, I think, not be wrong on the rest.

Gardiner speaks of "the few Bills" then passed. If the bills that were passed were so few, then the Houses themselves were to blame. For the King vetoed never a bill. I shall deal with this matter more fully in some pages on Eliot's perversions, on which he, perchance, had relied.

SUPPLY RECONSIDERED

We have stated in summary fashion our view of the Subsidies Bill. That view is not that of the Whigs. Let us, therefore, go into detail and consider the Whig view at length. To meet parliament, as we have seen, Charles was not only willing but anxious. We have his account of the matter put out in the following year; there is nothing improbable in it. In " a true, plain and clear Declaration of the Causes which moved His Majesty to assemble, and after enforced him to dissolve these Parliaments," we come on this pertinent passage : " When his Majesty by the death of his dear and royal father of ever blessed memory, first came to the Crown, he found himself engaged in a war with a potent enemy, not undertaken rashly, nor without just and honourable grounds,

[97] *Commons' Journals*, I, p. 808; *Fawsley Debates*, p. 66.
[98] *Fawsley Debates*, p. 153.

E

but enforced for the necessary defence of himself, and his dominions, for the support of his friends and allies, for the redeeming of the ancient honour of this nation, for the recovering of the patrimony of his dear sister, her consort, and their children, injuriously, and under colour of treaties and friendship taken from them; and for the maintenance of the true religion; and invited thereunto, and encouraged therein by the humble advice of both the Houses of Parliament, and by their large promises and protestations to his late Majesty, to give him full and real assistance in those enterprises which were of so great importance to this realm, and to the general peace and safety of all his friends and allies. But when his Majesty entered into a view of his treasure, he found how ill-provided he was to proceed effectually with so great an action, unless he might be assured to receive such supplies from his loving subjects as might enable him to manage the same.

"Hereupon his Majesty being willing to tread in the steps of his royal progenitors, for the making of good and whole-some laws for the better government of his people, for the right understanding of their true grievances, and for the supply of moneys to be employed for those public services, he did resolve to summon a Parliament with all convenient speed he might; and finding a former Parliament already called in the life of his father, he was desirous for the speedier dispatch of his weighty affairs, and gaining of time, to have continued the same without any alteration of the members thereof, had he not been advised to the contrary by his judges and council at law, for that it had been subject to question in law, which he desired to avoid. But as soon as possibly he could he summoned a new Parliament, which he did with much con-fidence and assurance of the love of his people, that those who not long before had with some importunity won his father to break off his former treaties with Spain, and to effect it had used the mediation of his now Majesty, being then Prince, and a member of the Parliament, and had promised in Parliament their uttermost assistance for the enabling of his late Majesty to undergo the war which they then foresaw might follow, would have assuredly performed it to his now Majesty, and would not have suffered him in his first enterprise of so great an expectation to have run the least hazard through their defaults." [99]

Charles inherited James's engagements and found himself, therefore, at war. Certain policies, he clearly believed, had been pressed on his father by parliament; they had made him their " mediator " and, foreseeing the war that might follow, had promised their " uttermost assistance." To enable them to grant that assistance and redeem their protestations and pledges was, in consequence, his primary purpose in calling the Houses together. For the uses of parliament were three-fold : " the making of good and wholesome laws for the better government of the people," " the right understanding of their true grievances," " the supply of moneys to be employed for those public services." Parliament thus had great functions; the King was no arbitrary monarch. The reader should note well such phrases, as plain and sincere as *gratuitous*.

All this is, I think, in accordance with his speech at the opening of parliament and that of the Lord Keeper, Williams. They asked, and asked frankly, for money; the matter they believed to be urgent. It is true that no figure was mentioned; it is true that no enemy was *named*. But the object was stated by Williams, and nothing so far could be plainer. Charles's principal reason, he stated, for calling the Houses together was " to let them understand the great engagements for the recovery of the Palatinate."

Though Charles's immediate object was thus, in a single word, money, " the making of good and wholesome laws " was by no means entirely forgotten. We have seen that the Lord Keeper told them, " His Majesty desires them to bestow this meeting on him, or rather on these actions; and the next shall be theirs, as long and as soon as they will, for domestic business." This is borne out by Mandeville's letter, from which we have already cited: " The King hath already professed it [the Parliament] is not to sit long, and if his errand were dispatched, which is for money, all other business

[99] *Bibliotheca Regia* (1659), p. 355; Rushworth, p. 406. " This present month of June " is referred to—in 1626.

should expect a new session, which he prefers to be as soon as they will, and then as long as the[y] will." [100]

They were summoned in spite of the plague; they were not to sit long on account of it. Charles himself made this quite clear. We have seen the position was such that a motion could be made in the Commons as early as June the 21st " to petition the King, to adjourn till Michaelmas, in respect of the plague," [101] which was followed at once by another " for removal to another place." [102] Both motions, however, were shelved.[103] There is reason for thinking that Charles in the earlier days of the session not only had then no intention of adjourning to Oxford or elsewhere but even disapproved of such schemes and expected the granting of money to be hastened by the spread of the plague. We find this in Mandeville's letter : " The infection so spreads as we must scatter shortly; yet the King means that argument shall urge for doing something instantly, for to another place he will not now adjourn it." The writer continues as follows : " The business of the higher House will be nothing till something come from the lower House; and in the lower House I perceive, if the most may have their wills, there will be nothing done at this time but these two, one for God, the other for the King : they have already pressed in matter of religion to have the laws put in execution—the priests and Jesuits to be banished—and for the King, to condescend quickly to give somewhat." [104] Whether Mandeville meant that the Commons had then no intention of dealing with the question of tonnage and poundage we cannot, I think, now determine.

[100] See p. 21, *supra*, and p. 18, n. 3, *supra*.

[101] *Commons' Journals*, I, p. 800 ; *Fawsley Debates*, p. 7.

[102] By Wansford ; *Fawsley Debates*, p. 8 ; *Commons' Journals*, I, p. 800.

[103] " Suppressed by order " (*Fawsley Debates*, p. 8) ; " not now to be put to the question " (*Commons' Journals*, I, p. 800).

[104] See p. 18, n. 3, *supra*. There were *rumours*, of course, of removal. See a letter dated June the 17th : " To-morrow his Majesty will be present in the upper house to begin the parliament, which is thought shall be removed to Oxford " (*Court and Times of Charles the First*, I, p. 31). And Williams suggested to Conway in writing on June the 13th the " propriety of opening the session privately, putting off the term, and removing the Parliament " (*Calendar of State Papers, Domestic Series*, 1625, 1626, p. 44).

Be that as it may, " to give somewhat " can only refer to a subsidy.

We have already seen that the Commons had only just sat down to business, when a motion was made for adjournment. Adjournment was tantamount clearly to refusing supplies to the King. Whether Mallory pleaded the plague to *prevent* an appropriation we cannot, at this date, be certain. It is at least far from unlikely in one who, beyond doubt, belonged to the Northern men grouped around Wentworth. Wentworth was opposed to the war, and we find him supporting the motion; indeed, he appears to have urged " that a Committee might be named to draw a petition for that purpose." [105]   But Phelips was perfectly definite. We find in the *Fawsley Debates:* " Mr. Mallery. To petition the King that we may be adjourned till Michael[mas]. This motion Sir William Stroude thought to divert by another for a Committee for petitions, and that one man might not be employed in the chair for that service but divers; but the former was seconded by Sir Robert Phillips. That it was no time, considering the sickness, to take upon us such businesses. A supply was propounded; but we ought rather to consider how we may supply the commonwealth. In the first place to look to the law of God. There was matter of fear in every part of the state. Before we think upon giving now we ought likewise to take an account of that which was last given, and because our time cannot possibly extend to all, we should rather desire his Majesty to be referred to some other time." [106] " That it was no time, considering the sickness, to take upon us such businesses " referred, I suppose, to Strode's motion. The *Journals* give Phelips as saying " Yet considerable, whether this time fit to receive petitions against Courts of Justice, etc." [107]   Phelips's far stronger statements are not to be found in the *Journals*. The words, " a supply was

[105] *Fawsley Debates,* p. 8.
[106] *Ibid.,* p. 7.
[107] *Commons' Journals,* I, p. 800; " Sir Ro. Phillips secondeth the motion :—Yet considerable, etc." " Motion," as the matter is reported, would appear to refer to Strode's motion. This, however, can hardly be right, if the *Fawsley Debates* are correct.

propounded," apparently refer to the speeches of Charles and of Williams at the opening.   Or else we must take them to bear their more natural and obvious meaning—a motion had been made in the House.   But no evidence of that is forth-coming.   Among those replying to Phelips was Heath, the Solicitor-General.   He referred in his speech to supply : " If we part now without doing anything it will weaken his [the King's] reputation more than can be restored by the grant of many subsidies.   He concluded, because our time could not be long, we should name a Committee to consider what was most necessary for the present, and to bend ourselves to that " [108]—in substance the motion by Alford, " for a Com-mittee of the whole House, to consider of the course fit to be holden, both for King and Kingdom." [109]   But nothing apparently came of it.   The motions for adjournment and removal—we know this for certain—were shelved ; but we learn of no *positive* conclusion to the speeches that centred around them.

When the House met again on the morrow, a Committee of Grievances was moved for.[110]   Then Alford repeated his motion—" to have a Committee, to consider of what course we shall take in all business this Parliament." [111]   Sir Benjamin Rudyerd, who followed, commended the King at some length.   The debate led to various motions and roamed over various topics, and supply was occasionally mentioned. In the end, as we read in the *Journals,* " *Resolved,* A Com-mittee of the whole House, to-morrow morning, Mr. Speaker sitting by, to consider of all the foresaid propositions, and of whatsoever else shall be offered." [112]   Then we come to a blank in the *Journals.*   But we find in the *Fawsley Debates* for the 23rd June, the next day : " *Eodem die* at the Great Committee concerning religion and supply.   The matter of religion and the question for supply stood committed to the

[108] *Fawsley Debates,* p. 8.
[109] *Commons' Journals,* I, p. 800.
[110] *Commons' Journals,* I, p. 800 ;   *Fawsley Debates,* p. 9.
[111] *Commons' Journals,* I, p. 800.
[112] *Ibid.,* I, p. 801.

whole House, wherein religion was to have the first place." [113]
We, therefore, I think, had good ground, when we drew this
important conclusion : proposals concerning supply had been,
totidem verbis, ruled out, till all matters affecting " religion "
had first been sent up to the Lords.

I mentioned the blank in the *Journals.* No reason for this
seems forthcoming; and none has been ever suggested. But
why were no entries then made? Did the Commons, to put
it quite plainly, intend thus to cover their tracks?

Thus we come to the last day of June and what followed
the motion by Seymour. We need not repeat the facts
here.[114] But an act for the grant of two subsidies was read
a first time on the 4th and a second time on the next day and
committed to the House as a whole. On the 8th it was read
a third time and was passed and sent up to the Lords, where it
passed the same day through all stages.[115]

The arguments Phelips put forward deserve a few moments'
attention, as Seymour's are not upon record.[116] And first for
his principal point : " There is no engagement; the promises
and declarations of the last Parliament were in respect of a
war; we know yet of no war nor of any enemy." Admittedly,
then, there were promises made in the previous parliament—
made in respect of a war. But why in that case " no engage-

[113] *Fawsley Debates,* p. 16.
[114] We may mention here one or two blunders. Forster would have us
suppose Sandys did not sit at all in this parliament. " Sir Edwin Sandys
lost Kent because of the rumours that he was to be made secretary in
Calvert's place, though the office had been given to Sir Albert Morton."
" He took little part in public affairs after James's death." See Forster's
Sir John Eliot, I, p. 227. The *Cambridge Modern History* has this: " In
vain the courtiers urged the need of an unusually large grant " (IV,
p. 259). So is history too frequently made. Gardiner thinks Phelips's
motion was really an " amendment " to Seymour's. If the *Fawsley
Debates* are correct, he was merely supporting a motion already put
forward by others. " Most . . . pitched upon two entire subsidies "
precedes the report of his speech. See Gardiner, *History of England,* V,
p. 347, and *Fawsley Debates,* p. 31.
[115] *Commons' Journals,* I, pp. 802, 803, 806; *Lords' Journals,* III,
p. 460. Sir John Corbett, member for Yarmouth, told Mead upon
July 11 " that they had granted two subsidies (before any such thing was
propounded from the King), and that freely without any condition of
bestowing it; but all recusants to pay four subsidies or double to
Protestants " (Mead to Stuteville, *Court and Times of Charles the First,*
I, p. 42). For the last point see *Fawsley Debates,* p. 33.
[116] See the *Fawsley Debates,* pp. 30, 31–2.

ment "? " Engagement " must mean " obligation," for
plainly it cannot mean " promise." Thus the passage would
seem to mean this : the Houses were not yet " engaged,"
since they knew not as yet of a war ; no war, then no obligation ; the time, otherwise, was not yet, when the carrying out
of their pledges could well be demanded by Charles. But the
Houses " knew yet of no war." What is this but incredible
sophistry? Spain, we have seen, was not *named* ; but Phelips
went on to inquire " what account is to be given of 20,000
men, of many thousand pounds of treasure, which have been
expended without any success of honour or profit." If they
knew of no war and no enemy, how did they know of those
men, of those thousands of pounds thus expended? And
Phelips continued as follows : " It was not wont to be so
when God and we held together ; witness that glorious
Q[ueen], who with less supplies defended herself, consumed
Spain, assisted the Low Countries, relieved France, preserved
Ireland." While pretending to know of no war, he complained of the conduct of war. Indeed, " he concluded that
we should be suitors to the King to take these things into his
consideration, and to proceed in his government by a grave
and wise counsel." He ended by expressing a hope that " at
the return of the navy there will be better inducements "—
a hope, in other words, that the navy would provide better
reasons for giving by successful operations at sea. None the
less, " there was no cause for more." The man who thus
stated in June that he knew of no war and no enemy could
say upon August the 5th, " For our sins God brought upon us
the Spanish treaties, from which was induced the Prince's
journey, and of that the effect is this war." [117] It is also, I
think, worth attention that, according to the *Fawsley Debates,*
he said nothing about the Palatinate.

Was Phelips sincere? " They diminish the King," so he
said, " that think money can give him reputation," as though
he had but to be penniless and his name would stand highest
in Europe. " The hearts of his subjects are his greatest
honour and reputation." Would " the hearts of his subjects,"

[117] *Fawsley Debates,* p. 80.

however, suffice to recover the Palatinate? James, as we noticed in passing, had already told the two Houses, " It is not sufficient to have the hearts of my subjects." [118] Was Phelips indulging in parody? Then the compliments paid to King Charles : " There was never any king upon whom there were fewer notes of vice, and we ever be thankful subjects." Gardiner observes in his *History* of Phelips's opening remarks that " to Charles at least " they " must have sounded like bitter irony." [119] To Charles, one conceives, the whole speech must have sounded like something quite different. After painting the state of the realm at the time of the new King's accession in terms even Gardiner allows to be " somewhat exaggerated," it made this most impudent claim—" there cannot be a greater argument of our love than that we are at this time contented to lay aside the right of the subject." How this spirit of patience and forbearance was evinced but a few days later in the matter of tonnage and poundage we had some occasion to see.

But a far greater issue remains, more important than this or that argument advanced in debate in the House. We must emphasize here certain points we have already touched upon briefly. The " courtiers " had never expected supply would come up on that date. A surprise was, in fact, sprung upon them, and few could be found in their places till, the matter being practically settled, intervention appeared to be useless. The Crown was effectively silenced. So far as we learn from the records, none spoke on the King's side but Rudyerd, who seems to have been a free lance. As he mentioned no definite sum, he at least can have had no instructions. " A division," as we now say, " was snatched." But " divers were provided to have spoken and meant to have urged for a larger proportion." Thus the making of definite proposals and the stating of the case for the Crown were effectively prevented by Seymour, who was probably acting with others, for Phelips, Coke, Wentworth and Sandys fell so readily in with his tactics. In a word, Charles was not to be heard. Why

[118] See p. 25, *supra.*
[119] V, p. 346.

resort to so mean a manoeuvre? And was the King's own case so strong that it must at all costs be suppressed?

And now let us listen to Gardiner. We read, if we turn to his *History*: "The Court party was taken by surprise. Many of its members were absent from the House; all of them had been left without instructions how such an emergency was to be met." [120] That is all he there says on that point. In the Preface to the *Fawsley Debates* he makes almost the same criticism: "The Courtiers, as is well known, were taken by surprise. They had no instructions, and they allowed the amended motion to be carried, as for two subsidies, without remonstrance." [121] It may be that no such "emergency" entered the mind of the King. Nor yet does that seem the right word. Intervention, "remonstrance" were useless. Moreover, the fact is suppressed that "divers were provided to have spoken," which means, in one word, were *instructed*—not, indeed, to meet "such an emergency" but (as was more to the purpose) to argue the case for the Crown and to "urge for a larger proportion."

In fairness to Gardiner at this point we have to make one reservation. In his Preface to the *Fawsley Debates* he admits that the vote had been snatched; besides, he cites Eliot's admission that "some art there was to extenuate the proportion," which amounts to the very same thing.[122] He is not so explicit in his *History*. He regrets "the manner in which the thing was done." He holds that "an event of such historical importance as a breach between the Crown and the House of Commons should not have been allowed to take place upon a sudden and unexpected motion, followed by a hasty vote." He argues, however, that "the step taken by the House under the guidance of Seymour and Phelips was certainly justifiable," while suggesting that "it would have spared itself much obloquy in the future, and would have conciliated much popular feeling at the time, if it had condescended"—how strange is that word "condescended"!—

[120] V, p. 345.
[121] p. viii.
[122] pp. vii and viii.

" to put its views and intentions into an address in vindication of its thoroughly legitimate position. That there was no ill intention is probable enough. Men who disliked voting money for questionable objects would be glad enough to escape from the necessity of entering into controversy with their sovereign, and would doubtless flatter themselves that, in voting two subsidies, they had done the King considerable service." [123] Here is not only much special pleading but what may be fairly described as " some art to extenuate " the facts. How far the step taken by the Commons can be held to be " thoroughly legitimate " readers themselves can determine in view of that House's engagements. But what we call " snatching a division " is now described somewhat more vaguely as " a sudden and unexpected motion, followed by a hasty vote." " That there was no ill intention is probable enough"—this, however, of Seymour and Phelips, of a shameless intrigue without precedent! How could such men as its authors " flatter themselves that, in voting two subsidies, they had done the King considerable service "? Who, indeed, that reads Phelips's speech could suppose that he wished for one moment to do some " considerable service "? Not to add that on June 21 he " rather desired his Majesty to be referred to some other time." So far was the House, then, from failing to " vindicate " a rightful position from a lack of what is called " condescension," that it seems to be only too plain it was bent on evading the issues.

Gardiner condemns Charles's methods. He writes in his Preface as follows: " Whatever the reason may have been, the reins were allowed to drop from his hands. The Commons were invited in general terms by the Lord Keeper to give money. But how much was wanted, and what it was wanted for, they were not told." [124] " As far as the King was concerned, the reins were thrown upon the horse's neck, to take which road he pleased." [125] Again, we read thus in the *History*: " On the 21st the Commons proceeded to business.

[123] V, p. 347.
[124] p. v.
[125] p. vii.

There could be no doubt that precedent as well as ordinary courtesy demanded an explicit statement on the King's behalf of the amount of the proposed expenditure and of the reasons upon which the demand was founded. With the last Parliament James had entered into a direct engagement to take the Commons into his confidence when they next met. Whether, if Charles had told the truth, he would have satisfied the Houses, may well be questioned. He preferred to tell them nothing at all. Not a minister rose in his place in the Lords or Commons to say how much was wanted, or to explain in what way the supply, if it were voted, would be spent. Charles threw the reins about the neck of Parliament and expected it to follow his call. Silence under such circumstances, whether the result of a deliberate purpose or, as is more likely, of mere youthful inexperience and ignorance of human nature, was in itself the worst of policies." [126] Again : " What Charles expected the Commons to do as soon as they had relegated their religious grievances to the House of Lords it is impossible to say. Supply stood next in order to be treated of ; but though twelve days of the session had passed away, giving him time to reflect on the attitude of the Commons, he had taken no steps to explain to them the real meaning of the vague demands which he had made in his opening speech." [127] Once more : " Charles's want of confidence in the House was thus met by a vote which was practically a vote of want of confidence in his advisers." [128] What ground can be found for such charges ?

Go back to the opening of parliament. Did not the King's preparations " meet all in one centre, the Palatinate " ? Was not, indeed, this his object in calling the Houses together," to let them understand the great engagements for the recovery of the Palatinate " ? Was it not, then, for this object that money was urgently needed ? The King would explain his engagements, and a statement of accounts would be rendered.

[126] V, p. 339. Note that Gardiner insists on "engagements," where the Crown was concerned, not the Commons, although there was now a new parliament.

[127] V, p. 344.

[128] V, p. 347.

Far from "telling them nothing at all," Charles would "take" the House "into his confidence," supplying that "explicit statement" required by the nature of things. What other construction, in truth, could be placed on the Lord Keeper's language? "Divers were provided to have spoken and meant to have urged for a larger proportion," when the Commons debated supplies. But if Charles's intentions were such, we have seen how their leaders contrived on the last day of June to defeat them. The King's "want of confidence" was it? For "confidence" read "opportunity." But Gardiner suggests that the King should have seized on some earlier occasion: "he had taken no steps to explain to them the real meaning," and so on.

This brings us at once to the point *when* a statement could thus have been made. What occurred upon June 21 we have already stated at length. The motion for adjourning the Houses would come as a surprise to the ministers. Phelips himself had admitted it was "rare, at the beginning of a Parliament, to petition to be put off." [129] According to Gardiner's account, "Whilst the House was still hesitating what to do, an unexpected motion was brought forward." [130] "Unexpected" it was—by the Crown—but I know of no reason for thinking the Commons were "still hesitating," as though they expected a statement as soon as they sat down to business. And would they, indeed, have allowed—not to say, sympathetically handled—an attempt to bring on a decision, when even the appointment of Committees, excepting the Committee for Privilege, had not then so much as been mentioned? Nor could a debate such as that which took place upon Mallory's motion have provided a fitting occasion for explicit demands for large sums. Not thus could a motion for adjournment, which may have been prompted entirely and was certainly inspired in large measure by a wish to refuse all assistance, be successfully met by the Court. The same arguments appear to apply to the sitting of June 22, which, in fact, did no more than continue the previous

[129] *Commons' Journals*, I, p. 800; see p. 31, *supra*.
[130] V, p. 340.

morning's debate. From the 23rd June to the 30th no chance
for a statement would offer; questions of supply, we have
seen, were not to be so much as raised till "religion" was out
of the way. The probable fate of a message we learn from
a subsequent instance. For Nethersole wrote of a message
received from the King four years later: "It fell to the
ground, because it was ordered before, that the matter of
religion should have precedence." [131] This trick could be
played more than once.

We may, therefore, conclude, as I think, that what
Gardiner has called the King's "silence" arose not from
any "want of confidence" nor yet from "mere youthful
inexperience." Had the latter, indeed, been the reason, more
shame on the Commons to exploit it! [132]

That a statement on Charles's behalf and a plea for a
definite figure would have altered the course of events must,
I think, be much open to doubt. On the one hand, the
measures adopted for the purpose of "snatching a division"
would suggest that the parliamentary leaders much feared
the effects of a statement. On the other, a section of the
House were at heart indisposed to grant anything. Phelips,
again, is reported as saying on the 30th June: "But it will
be most for his [the King's] honour that what we do come
freely from us." [133] And how, we may ask, had James fared?
His experience was far from encouraging. He asked them the
previous year for six subsidies, twelve fifteenths; three
subsidies, three fifteenths—less than half—did the lower house
vote him.

GARDINER ON TONNAGE AND POUNDAGE

Now let us turn for a moment to Gardiner's account of
this bill. It would seem to be sadly inadequate—even
ostentatiously negligent. No mention is made of Heath's

---

[131] Sir Francis Nethersole to Elizabeth, Queen of Bohemia, January 28,
1629; *Calendar of State Papers, Domestic Series*, 1628–9, p. 459; see
also p. 158.

[132] He makes the King wholly responsible up till the 8th of July. Then
the Duke takes the place of the King; Coke is "Buckingham's mouth-
piece," and so on.

[133] *Fawsley Debates*, p. 32.

motion, though there lay the heart of the matter. His part
is dismissed in one sentence : " In spite of Heath's opposition,
the House resolved to grant tonnage and poundage for one
year only." Not a word of Heath's actual proposal, not a
word of " the advice of the Lords." Then Gardiner continues
as follows : " The Bill thus drawn was carried up to the
House of Lords and was there read once. It is not necessary
to suppose a deliberate intention to defeat it, but neither, it
would seem, was there any desire to hurry it on ; and the Bill
was swept away by the tide of events which brought the
session to a hurried close." [134] But *why* was there no " desire "
in the Lords' House " to hurry it on " ? And *why* was it not
taken up, when the Houses again met at Oxford ? We find
this also in a note in regard to the original authorities : " In
addition to the scanty notices in the *Journals,* we have for this
Parliament Eliot's *Negotium Posterorum,* which has been
edited by Dr. Grosart, and the Fawsley MS. belonging to
Sir R. Knightley, which I have edited for the Camden
Society. I shall refer to the latter as *Fawsley Debates.* Unless
there is any special necessity for referring to one particular
source, it will be understood that what I say in the text is
founded on these authorities. The further volume of notes
taken by Eliot I shall give as *Eliot Notes."* [135] Eliot's account
of this bill in *Negotium Posterorum* conflicts on the most vital
point—or the King's alleged use of the veto—with the *Journals*
and the *Fawsley Debates ;* yet of this there is no hint in
Gardiner.

As is Gardiner's account of the bill, so is also his plea for
the Commons. " Phelips," he says, " who succeeded Erle,
carried the debate into another region. He moved that the
Bill ' might so be passed as not to exclude the question of
other impositions.' The old quarrel which had been
smothered in 1621 and 1624, when the Commons were look-

---

[134] *History,* V, p. 365. Contrast Mr. Fletcher's opinion, which seems to
me equally dubious : " The Lords, taking the natural view that this was
an unnecessary irritation, would almost certainly have amended or
thrown out the Bill, had Parliament not been dissolved before they could
do so " *(Introductory History of England,* p. 281). The peers had had
plenty of time to amend or reject.

[135] *Ibid.,* V, p. 338, note 2.

ing forward to co-operation with the Crown in war, was
certain to break out afresh when there was no longer any
such prospect. Even if there had been no change in this
respect, it is hard to see how the question could have been
avoided when the beginning of a new reign opened up the
whole subject by the introduction of a new Bill for the grant
of tonnage and poundage. Phelips took up a position which
was logically unassailable. If the King, he said, possessed the
right of imposing duties upon merchandise at his own
pleasure, why was Parliament asked to grant that which
belonged already to the Crown? In spite of Heath's opposition, the House resolved to grant tonnage and poundage for
one year only. There would thus be time to consider the
questions which had been raised." [136] This defence is, I think,
vitiated by more than one mistaken assumption. It implies
that in no other way than by passing a temporary measure
could " the rights of the Commons " be saved and the questions at issue considered, while, as soon as we recognize clearly
that the " rights " in this matter were twofold, the argument
propounded by Phelips is seen to be destitute of force. The
position was somewhat too subtle for Phelips's clear-cut
distinctions. Heath was prepared to admit that the House
had its " rights " " in those questions." But the Crown had
its " rights," in like manner—rights that, according to Forster,
no other than Eliot himself was to credit the Commons with
saving! Long and formal renewal of the customs had
created crown property in them.

Heath appealed to tradition and precedent, when he spoke
of " so many descents." Though unbroken for so many
reigns, they were now to be thus set aside. Notwithstanding,
when it suited their purpose, the enemies of Charles and of
Buckingham could make a great play with their precedents.
What said one member at Oxford, according to Eliot himself?
" ffirst, ther has beene an obiection made against insisting on
ould presidents, & that we should not make them Gods, wch
in part was awnswear'd, that they were venerable, though not
idolls : but further, presidents are the life & rule of parlia-

ments, noe other warrant being for the parliament it self, for the authorities it pretends to, then the extent vse & practise, wch is drawne out by presidents. & should not then parliaments be carefull to preserve that rule inviolable, to make it constant like it self? in other Courts differenc of presidents are badges of distemper & weakness in those times, much more would it be in this great Court of Parliament, wch being the rectifier of others, should this waie doe it self; & if that straie or wander by wch the rest are guided, who shall then rectifie & reduce it? but even those that speak against them, doe most magnifie & endear them, when they thinke them vsefull to them selves." [137] To be sure, "even those that speak against them do most magnify and endear them, when they think them useful to themselves." Disregard for a moment the decision that was given in the Court of Exchequer; and the rights of the Crown and the Commons in the matter of tonnage and poundage had "no other warrant" than precedent.

ELIOT AND FORSTER ON TONNAGE AND
POUNDAGE

In view of the preceding sections the account Sir John Eliot gives of the tonnage and poundage bill merits surely a few moments' notice. It throws a strange light on its author. Let me, first of all, quote the whole passage, since Grosart's edition of Eliot is not to be readily come by and, as we shall see very shortly, we cannot rely upon Forster. Here is the statement *verbatim*, the spelling and so forth unaltered:

" the next thing w[ch] remayn'd was the bill for the two subsidies that were given, w[ch] likewise being past the house of Commons, & that intimated to the K[ing], it produc'd a message from his ma[tie], w[ch] shortlie after followd it, that gave a generall hope & confidence of a speedie conclusion & recess.

" the message was delivered by the Lo. Keeper, the K[ing]

---

[137] *Negotium Posterorum*, II, p. 98; inaccurately cited by Forster *(ibid.,* I, p. 434). The speaker, says Forster, was Littleton, "called up by a speech from Sir Humphrey May," and the date, he says, August the 11th. May spoke on the 10th, not 11th. As is clear from the *Fawsley Debates*, it was Sherland, who spoke on the 12th (pp. 125, 148).

F

being then retir'd to Hampton Court from the danger of the infection; & it came as addrest to both houses, that his ma^{tie} receav'd great satisfaction & contentment in their guift, both for the forme and matter, it comming as an ernest of their loves. that he tooke into consideration their safties, yea more than his owne in respect of the danger of the sickness still increasing; & that, when he should hear the Commons were readie, though he would not hasten them in anie thing, he would not defer one minute for anie reason to putt an end to that sitting by his presence or otherwise. this message & the time wrought soe effectuallie wth all men as what they desird, [that] they easilie did beleeve, & therupon dispos'd themselves presentlie to retire.

" their grant they sawe accepted, & all thinges left to the discretion of the house. the business then depending was not much, new they presumd would not be receavd; those few questions that remaynd were of noe great importance & most of them but formall, so as they now conceavd noe necessitie of their presence, & that their non-attendance was dispensable. in this confidence the greatest part went off, hardlie were the Commons a fourth part of their number, and those that staid, resolv'd, wth all the hast they could to followe those were gone. to that end they tooke a survey of their business. in the first ranck they plac'd the bill of tonnage and poundage, wch then remaynd imperfect, & to this they gave the first consideration for dispatch, & soe a second reading. it was drawne in the usuall forme, as formerlie it had beene in the daies of K[ing] J[ames] for the like terme of life, & in such latitude as to him; at wch some exceptions were then made, & motions for change & alteration, upon wch it was referd for the better discussion & debate to the grand Com^{tee} of the house, into w^{ch}, the Speaker leaving his chaire, they presentlie resolvd themselves. some did object, in that, the exactions of the officers, & the inequalitie of the customes then requird, & urg'd thereon a necessitie for the marchantes to have a new booke of rates, to settle & compose it, wch could not be prepar'd in soe short a time & sitting. others alledgd the pretermitted customes, grounded upon the misconstruction of that lawe, wch ought to be examind likewise, & the lawes that then remayn'd were thought to be incapable of that worke. therfore on these reasons they inferd a desire for a limitation in the act, & that it might but continue for one year, against wch time, these difficulties being resolvd, they might againe renew it wth a larger extension & continuance. others to this added the question of impositions in the generall and cravd a speciall care not to have that excluded. the elder times were mention'd to note the former grantes, wherin though ther were collected a great varietie & difference, yet all were wthin the limitation of some years: sometimes for one, sometimes for two, but seldome above three, & that in ye best raignes & governmentes & to the wisest princes; never for life till towardes the end of H[enry] 6. in whose beginninges also it had had other limitations & restraintes, & for the time a less extent & latitude. upon wch likewise it was concluded, for a present alteration in that pointe. the King's Councell opposd this wth much sollicitation and indeavor, & urg'd the distast it might occasion having somanie descentes held constant in that forme; all the raigne of K[ing] J[ames], all the raigne of Q[ueen] E[lisabeth] & soe to Q[ueen] M[ary] E[dward] 6. H[enry] 8. H[enry] 7, & beginning in that raigne, not the most deserving of all others, of H[enry] 6. the hopes & merittes of the K[ing] were compard wth all his ancestors & it was prest as a preiudice therin if the grant should then be limitted, having beene absolut to the others. It was consented that a proviso should be added for the saving of those rightes: [138] but in other things it was cravd wholie to be free, that the K[ing] might not thinke himself lessend in estimation. this argument was much forc't for the perswasion of the house, as after it was doubted to be elswher [139] made their preiudice: but it prevail'd not against those other considerations that were rais'd, upon wch it was concluded for a limitation & restraint.

"the bill thus past that house had it's transition to the Lords, wher it receavd like favor & dispatch but was not

[138] Clearly the "rights" of the Commons. This agrees with the *Fawsley Debates.* See p. 35, *supra.*

[139] Does "elsewhere" here mean "in the Lords"?

made a lawe, wanting the *Roy le vuit,* wch being denied it, shewd what must be look'd for." [140]

Such is Eliot's account of the matter. I pass over here the mistakes in regard to the Subsidies Bill and proceed to the main points at issue. And, first, let us note that, so far from its having been vetoed by Charles, the Tonnage and Poundage Bill had been read only once in the Lords. Yet this statement about the royal veto is surely no casual assertion, for twice does its author repeat it. "The bill of tonnage & pondage was at rest in the custodie of the Lords, & noe knowledg, but by divination could be had, how it would speed after wth the K[ing]." [141] Once more : "The bill of tonnage & pondage was reiected & yet those levies made, wch was held an indication of more love to the waies of power then right." Not only was this bill rejected ; the veto was used somewhat freely ! "The lawes that had approbation were not manie & the choise of them not great. that against recusantes was not past, & in all, their number was but seven." [142] Was "that against recusants" the bill, for I know not what else it can be, thus described in the *House of Lords' Journals* : "An act for the Explanation of a Branch of the Statute, made in the Third Year of the Reign of our late Sovereign Lord King James, intituled, An Act for the better discovering and repressing of Popish Recusants "? If so, it was read a first time in the Lords upon July the 1st, a second upon August the 10th ; but it never came up for third reading. In a word, as a matter of history, no bill whatsoever was vetoed.[143]

Two other points in this statement conflict with well-ascertained facts. "Hardly were the Commons a fourth part

---

[140] *Negotium Posterorum* (ed. by Grosart), I, p. 92. The full title of this very rare book, which was published in 1881, is *An Apology for Socrates and Negotium Posterorum : by Sir John Eliot (1590–1632), Now for the first time printed : From the Author's MSS. at Port Eliot.* But a hundred copies were printed, and those for subscribers only. This book does not seem to be mentioned in the fairly extensive bibliography in the *Cambridge Modern History,* IV, p. 884. Yet its influence has, thanks to John Forster, been widespread and wholly pernicious.

[141] *Ibid.,* I, p. 109. See p. 78, *infra.*

[142] *Negotium Posterorum,* I, p. 125. "Respited," Forster, for "rejected" *(Sir John Eliot* [1864], I, 309). In addition to his other deficiencies he failed to decipher his text.

[143] *Lords' Journals,* III, pp. 451, 485, 490.

of their number." [144]   Yet the *Journals* record a division on the morning of July the 5th; the subject was Wentworth's election; two hundred and twenty-seven voted; this *followed* the vital debate on the question of tonnage and poundage.[145] On Eliot's basis the Commons must, therefore, have numbered a thousand!

Our suspicions are increased, when we turn to what Eliot says of the lawyers: "the lawyers that then remained were thought to be incapable of that work," for "lawes," I presume, must be "lawyers." Suffice it to cite from the *Journals* two entries for July the 6th:

"L. 2ᵃ. AN Act against—.

Committed to Sir *Edw. Coke*, Mr. *Glanvyle*, Sir *Tho. Middleton*, Mr. *Alford*, Sir *Jo. Stradling*, all the Lawyers of the House, Sir *Francis Barrington*, Sir *Ben. Rudyard*, Sir *Wm. Pitt* : And all, that will come, to have Voice :— *Friday*, Two Clock, Court Wards."

"L. 3ᵃ. An Act, that this Session of Parliament shall not determine, by his Majesty's Royal Assent unto One or more Acts of Parliament.

After the Reading of this Bill, Doubts conceived; and thereupon Mr. Solicitor, Mr. *Glanvyle*, Sir *Ro. Phillippes*, Sir *Francis Seymor*, Sir *Jo. Stradling*, Mr. *Cage*, Mr. *Alford*, and all the Lawyers of the House, directed to go into the Committee Chamber." [146]

Several of the principal lawyers remained in the House to the end.

Moreover, according to Eliot, "the business then depending was not much, new they presumed would not be received;

---

[144] Gardiner repeats this strange statement in his *History* (V, p. 349). His chronology seems, at this point, I may add, to be somewhat confused, as he speaks of the Yorkshire election, declared null and void on the 5th, as a matter "already decided," when Williams brought the message from the King about ending the session on the 4th.

[145] *Commons' Journals*, I, p. 803 (Yeas, 94; Noes, 133). Members may have hurried away *after* July the 5th or the 6th. Charles himself is reported by Heath as remarking on July the 8th, "I understand your House grows very empty" (*Fawsley Debates*, p. 62). See *Scrinia Reserata*, II, p. 13; Locke to Carleton on July 9 in the *Fawsley Debates*, p. 154.

[146] *Commons' Journals*, I, p. 804.

those few questions that remained were of no great importance and most of them but formal." Could the question of
tonnage and poundage be called one "of no great importance"? If not, does he mean that the matter had escaped
the attention of the Commons or at least of that mythical
majority, that swiftly and suddenly vanished, or else that the
members of the House had no knowledge nor anticipation of
the questions that forthwith arose? But those questions, in
fact, had been stirred in debate upon June 22.[147]

We are not as yet done with the problems arising from
Eliot's statement. Why that unnecessary haste? We shall
seek for an answer in vain. Why the question assumed this
importance, so sudden and so unexpected, when, if Eliot's
account is reliable, the principal lawyers had gone and three-
fourths of the House had departed, we are wholly unable to
discover.

If, however, we confine out attention to those statements
in Eliot's account, which at least are not certainly false, we
should yet make some obvious comments. The Commons'
original purpose was to limit in "extension and continuance"
the granting of tonnage and poundage. First of all it should
be for one year, then, it might be, for two or for three—
never more at the most than for three. Thus the aim of the
parliamentary leaders is only too plainly disclosed. Then,
the difficulties and grievances alleged in the matter of a new
book of rates, "the exactions of the officers" and so on are
not, as I conceive, to the point. Were they not to be allowed
to stand over? If, therefore, they nowise precluded the
passage of a bill through the Commons for a temporary grant
of the customs, so neither did they stand in the way of the
passage into law of a bill for the granting of the customs for
life. They could always be "saved" or reserved.

And now let us turn for a moment to Forster's report of
this matter. "The charges," he says, "most often and with
greatest apparent show of reason, brought against the first
parliament of Charles the First, by the favourers or advocates
of that prince, have turned upon the alleged niggardliness

---

[147] *Fawsley Debates,* p. 12.

with which, during a war to which the preceding parliament had been a strong consenting party, they doled out supplies that it had never been usual, even in time of peace, to stint at the opening of a reign; and, above all, upon the affront offered to the young sovereign by the proposed limitation to one year of the grant of tonnage and poundage which his predecessors had enjoyed for life. So much, it has always been said, was this resented, that the lords refused not merely to pass but even to entertain the bill. As to this last charge, it will be seen that Eliot puts the matter in a new light. The bill when first introduced renewed the grant for life, but it was not laid on the table until nearly three-fourths of the members, believing that all matters of supply had been voted, and alarmed by the advancing ravages of the plague, had quitted London for their country houses. Several questions then arose as to the new book of rates, and as to irregularities in collection; which, in the absence from the house of the principal lawyers, led of necessity to the proposed limitation, not as a permanent but as a temporary measure. Every supposed right of the monarch was at the same time carefully protected; and so far were the lords from refusing to entertain, that they had actually passed the bill, when the royal assent to it was refused." [148]

In another place, " Scarcely," says Forster, " had the house thus quickly cleared itself of three-fourths of its members, however, when one subject assumed suddenly an importance not expected. The bill for tonnage and poundage had been introduced in the usual form with the subsidy bill; but, upon the second reading coming on before that fragment of a house, such strong reasons presented themselves against the ordinary course of procedure as to lead to the suggestion, first made by Sir Francis Seymour, which has raised against this parliament its sharpest assailants. It will nevertheless appear to us, as here explained by Eliot, both justifiable and natural. The matter is too important not to be described in his exact words. The bill, he says, ' was drawne in the usuall forme, as formerlie it had been in the daies of King James; for the

like terme of life and in such latitude as to him. At which
some exceptions were then made, and motions for change
and alteration; upon which it was referr'd, for the better
discussion and debate, to the grand committee of the house,
into which, the Speaker leaving his chair, they presentlie
resolv'd themselves. Some did object, in that, the exactions
of the officers, and the inequalitie of the customs then
required; and urg'd therein a necessitie for the marchantes to
have a new book of rates, to settle and compose it; which
could not be prepared in so short a time and sitting. Others
alleged the pretermitted customs, grounded upon the misconstruction of that lawe, which ought to be examined likewise; *and the lawyers that then remayn'd were thought to be
incapable of that worke.* Therefore, on these reasons, they
infer'd a desire for a limitation in the act, and that it might
but continue for one year; against which time, those difficulties being resolv'd, *they might againe renew it with a larger
extension and continuance.* Others to this added the question
of impositions in the generall, and crav'd a special care not to
have that excluded. The elder times were mentioned to note
the former grants, wherin, though there were collected a
great varietie and difference, yet all were within the limitation of some years. Sometimes for one, sometimes for two,
seldome above three, and that in the best raignes and govern-
ments, and to the wisest princes: *but never for life till
towards the end of Henry VI,* in whose beginnings also it had
other limitations and restraints, and for the time a less extent
and latitude. Upon which likewise it was concluded for a
present alteration in that pointe. The king's councell oppos'd
this with much sollicitation and indeavor, and urg'd the distaste it might occasion, having so many descents held constant
in that forme. The hopes and meritts of the king wer com-
par'd with all his ancestors; and it was prest as a prejudice
therein if the grant should then be limited, having been
absolute to the others. *It was thereuppon consented that a
proviso should be added for the saving of those rights;* and
in this forme the bill past that house, and had its transition
to the lords, wher it receav'd like favor and dispatch; but was

not made a law, wanting the *roy le veut ; which being denied
it, showed what must be lookt for.'* [149]

Let the reader compare Forster's version with the version
I quoted from Grosart. "The matter is too important,"
says Forster, "not to be described in his exact words." Yet,
to pass over all minor questions, whole clauses are simply
omitted. Moreover, in one of the clauses the word "thereupon" has been added. Upon this particular sentence and
the meaning that he places upon it Forster's case for the
Commons is founded. The word "thereupon," as thus
added, ensures that it bears his own meaning. "Those
rights" must have been the King's rights, while the text
means the rights of the Commons. So much for Sir John's
"exact words." I say nothing at all of his spelling.[150]

Forster writes thus about Hume: "Mr. Hume's most
flagrant misstatements could not have been made if he would
have troubled himself a little oftener to leave his sofa, and
mount the ladder, in the advocates' library; and what
Mr. Nicholas Harding said of his *History* when the first
(Stuart) portion of it appeared, that the journals of the
houses would settle his facts, is applicable still to many others
as well as to him." [151] The *Journals* would have settled such
questions as that of the use of the veto. Did Forster consult
the *Lords' Journals?* If so, he must surely have known that
no bill whatsoever was vetoed. If not, then he stands self-
condemned. He was also, it seems, quite familiar with
Hacket's biography of Williams. He three times refers to
the paper in which the Lord Keeper took credit for "staying"
certain bills in the Lords, that for tonnage and poundage

---

[149] *Sir John Eliot*, I, p. 292. The italics are Forster's.

[150] Of his own extracts Forster observes: "The reader may rely with
perfect confidence on the scrupulous precision and accuracy with which
all that is essential in this remarkable manuscript will thus be laid before
him" *(ibid.,* I, p. 212). And Gardiner has also remarked: "For
ordinary readers, the very full extracts [of the *Negotium*] which he
[Forster] has printed are quite sufficient. Nothing in fact, except of a
very microscopic nature, has been omitted in his selections or his
abbreviations" (Preface to the *Fawsley Debates*, p. ii). As he also
thanked Forster for the loan of his copy of Eliot's manuscript, one must
suppose he was judging the extracts themselves by that copy.

[151] *Ibid.,* I, p. 411, note.

being one.[152] Could he, then, have believed that the bill, as
he tells us, was vetoed by Charles? Of such fictions are
popular histories too often composed in our time. J. R. Green
has repeated this fiction in what is, perhaps, the best known
and most popular history of England.[153] So error takes root,
gets repeated, established, and mightily flourishes.

Just a word upon Forster's own summary. Compare it
with Eliot's statement, as it stands mutilated in Forster. What
can we say of ascribing " the proposed limitation, not as a
permanent but as a temporary measure," to a number of
technical questions that only the lawyers could solve? That
the grant for one year was proposed " as a temporary
measure " was true. But the Commons had made up their
minds they would never again grant for life.

ELIOT AND BUCKINGHAM

Something, I think, must be said of the interview Eliot
tells us he had with the Duke in July. I should, on the whole,
have ignored it but that Gardiner accepts it as history and
comments at some length upon it and makes much of
Buckingham's motives.[154] First, let me quote the whole
passage as Grosart's edition transcribes it : [155] " Hitherto all
things had succeeded to the intentions of that house, noe
interruptions had beene raisd by the influenc of State. those
few publicke things then treated of, had a free way of
preparation, though some intimations had beene given that
their conclusions would not answeare it, but those had less in
credit, then of truth, and the satisfaction was presum'd to be
equall to the hope. From the confidence of Mountague &
that business, some seedes of ielosie were emergent, but noe
more. all things els had a sure shew & promise. the bill of
tonnage and pondage was at rest in the custodie of the Lords,
& noe knowledg, but by divination could be had, how it
would speed after wth the K[ing]. the best was still expected

---

[152] See *Sir John Eliot*, I, pp. 178, 231, 285.
[153] *A Short History of the English People* (1875), p. 481.
[154] *History*, V, pp. 366ff.
[155] I give it here just as it stands, punctuation and spelling unaltered, as
very few readers, indeed, can get access to Grosart's edition.

as hope did make construction, wch alwaies has an inclination vnto flatterie.

"But heer a checke came in, as distractive as vnlook't for. the D[uke of Buckingham] who was the Eolus of that time, had cast an alteration in the aer; the windes were turnd, & all the former happiness must be shadow'd wth some new clouds & vapors he had rais'd. He comes from the K[ing], who was then at Hampton Court, wth a pretended order for a new motion of supply. this in all hast must be perform'd & his privado's were all sent for to receave instruction in the pointe. this was about twelve a clock at night, at his owne house, wher, by reason of the suddainness & unseasonableness of the time, manie were not present, nor such as had much iudgment, they commonlie being most attendant on such persons, who are most obnoxious to their humors. these did consent in all, who studied not to counsell but to please; & soe what affections he had brought, they did both heigthen & confirme. but in the morning when it was come to others, whose qualitie was more knowing and ingenuous, they, as they apprehended it to be fatall & prodigious, soe gave it demonstration to the D[uke]. & wth all their power oppos'd it, adding to argumentes, entreaties for the prevention of that evill, wch did impplie apparantlie dishonor to the K[ing], [&] danger to him. of this number (not to deprive anie man of his due) was Sr Humphry May, then Chancelor of the Dutchie, who, having travaild wth much industrie in that service, but in vaine, came in great hast to a gentleman whom he thought more powerfull wth the D[uke] & knew to be affectionat to the publicke, & him he importund to a new attempt & triall for staie or diversion of that worke. it was at Westminster wher he mett him, & near the time of the sitting of the Commons. the D[uke] was then at York house. the entercourse 'twas obiected, would be long. noe certaine period could be prescribd for conference, wch in soe great a difficultie was not likelie to be short; soe as the proposition to the Parliament might be made before the discourse were ended, & the travaile by that means fruitless and vnnecessarie. but to remove this doubt the chancelor vndertooke to stop the motion till he came. onlie he wisht him to hasten his returne, & in his talke to intimat that staie vnto the D[uke]. vpon this he makes his passage & address, & comming to York house, findes the D[uke] wth his Ladie yet in bed; but notice being given of his comming, the Dutchess rose & wthdrew into her cabanett, & soe he was foorthwth admitted & lett in. the first thing mention'd was the occasion, & the fear that was contracted from that ground. the next was the honor of the K[ing] & respect vnto his saftie, from both wch were deduc'd argumentes of disswasion. ffor the king's honor was rememberd, the acceptation that was made of the two subsidies wch were past, & the satisfaction then profest, wch the new proposition would impeach, either in truth or wisdome, & againe the small number of the Commons that remaynd, the rest being gone upon the confidenc of that overture, would render it an ambuscado & surprise; wch at noe time could be honorable towardes subiectes, less in the entrance of the Soveraigne. the rule for that was noted, *ut initia proveniant fama in ceteris est.* the necessitie likewise of that honor was observ'd, wthout wch noe prince was great, hardlie anie fortunat. & on these grounds a larger superstructure was imposd as occasionallie the conferenc did require. ffor his own saftie, manie things were said, some more fitt for vse, then for memorie & report. the generall disopinion was obiected, wch it would worke to him, not to have oppos'd it, whose power was knowne to all men; & that the command comming by him self, would render it as his act, of wch imputation what the consequence might be nothing but divinitie could iudge, men that are much in favor being obnoxious to much envie. To these, answears were returned though weake, yet such as implied noe yeelding, that the acceptation wch was made of the subsidies then granted, was but in respect of the affection to the K[ing], not for satisfaction to his business. that the absence of the Commons was their owne fault & error, & their neglect must not preiudice the State. that the honor of the K[ing] stood upon the expectation of the ffleet, whose designe would vanishe if it were not speedilie set foorth. monie ther was wanting for that worke, & therin the King's honor was ingagd, w^{ch}

must outweigh all considerations for himself. this resolution being felt, was a new waie attempted, to try if that might weaken it. & to that end was obiected the improbabilitie of success; & if it did succeed, the greater loss might follow it, by alienation of the affections of the subiectes, who being pleasd were a fountaine of supplie, wthout wch those streames would soone drie up. but nothing could prevaile, ther being divers argumentes spent in that, yet the proposition must proceed, wthout consideration of success, wherin was lodg'd this proiect, meerlie to be denied. this secret that treatie did discover, wch drew on others that supported it of greater weight & moment, shewing a conversion of the tide for the present. it gave that gentleman some wonder wth astonishment, who wth the seale of privacie clos'd vp those passages in silence, yet therin grounded his observations for the future that noe respect of persons made him desert his countrie.

" this labor, not mispent, had taken vp much time. two houres, at least, went into the treatie & discourse, wch wth the entercourse had soe wasted the forenoone as ther remayn'd but little at his comming backe to Westminster; wher the like difficultie had beene to retard the proposition for that time, it being putt (not as other messages from the K[ing] into the mouth of his councellors and great officers, wherof ther are never wanting in the Commons house too manie; but) by a speciall choise, to the discreation of another, as an indication of his preferment then at hand, who was great, in his opinion, wth that honor & imploiment, & labor'd, as a woman does wth child, in desire to bring it foorth. the success being ther imparted, the motion did proceed. for wch ther wanted not some fitness in that instrument. the man so chosen was Sr John Coke, raisd from a lowe condition to that title by the D[uke]. to him he had beene recommended by that ould courtier S^r ffoulke Grevill, vnder whom he had had his education as a scholler, & soe was his service & imploiment; but his conversation being wth bookes, & that to teach not studie them, men & business were subiectes wch he knew not, & his expressions were more proper for a schoole, then for a State & councell." [156]

[156] *Negotium Posterorum* (Grosart), I, p. 109.

" I do not," of all this says Gardiner, " see any reason to suppose that things happened in the main otherwise than he [Eliot] tells them, though his view of the position is evidently coloured by the misconception that the Commons had already done all that the King could reasonably ask, even from Charles's own point of view." [157] For my own part, I see several reasons for distrusting the whole of the story.

(1) First, in regard to the date. Coke spoke upon July the 8th. Thus the meeting, if it ever took place, must have taken place sometime that morning.

(2) Already, so Eliot tells us, " the bill of tonnage and poundage was at rest in the custody of the Lords, and no knowledge but by divination could be had how it would speed after with the King," which must mean it had now passed the Lords. But we know that on July the 8th it had not even gone to the Lords. It had not passed the lower house even, when Coke rose to speak on that date.[158]

(3) Buckingham, then, on the 7th, having left Hampton Court, where the King was, had summoned his so-called " privadoes " post-haste to a midnight meeting. But who would surmise from this tale that the Duke was that morning in London? And yet, as the *Journals* record, he had been in his place in the Lords [159]—for the first and last time in the session, except when the King had been present.[160]

(4) He was, then, at the Lords in the morning, left London for Hampton Court later, had an interview there with the King, when they reached a momentous decision, returned to York House the same night and found time to call " all his privadoes " to a meeting about 12 o'clock. I need, I think, hardly point out that no reason whatever is given for a course so precipitate and sudden, nor can we at all understand, if he had such grave business on hand, what could make him go out of his way to attend the Lord's House in the morning. Can a summons from Charles have come later?

---

[157] *History*, V, p. 366, note 2. We find a strange slip on this page, for " from York House " should be " *to* York House."
[158] *Commons' Journals*, I, p. 807.
[159] III, p. 459.
[160] June 18 and 20 ; see *Journals*.

(5) May and Eliot meet at Westminster " near the time of the sitting of the Commons." What time the House met on that morning the *Journals* themselves do not say. Seven or eight was no uncommon hour. When and how did May hear of the business? And when did he visit the Duke? For how long did he " travail " in vain? [161]

(6) The interview takes up much time—as the story goes, " two hours, at least." When Eliot returns to Westminster, but little remains of the forenoon. What business preceded Coke's statement? And how were the Commons employed? The *Journals* make reference only to the Subsidy Bill (the third reading), the sending of a message accepting a conference proposed by the Lords and the bringing of a bill from the Lords, of which even the title is blank.[162] Of these items the third is ignored by the writer of the *Fawsley Debates,* and he mentions no additional business.[163] The reading of the Subsidy Bill must have been but the barest formality. Can we suppose that such items took most of the time before mid-day?

(7) What followed Coke's elaborate statement? The speech, without doubt, was a long one. That fact could be fairly inferred from the notes upon which we have drawn, were it not that Locke tells us for certain.[164] Coke made a like statement at Oxford, which was, he says, " near an hour long." [165] His proposal was seconded by Beecher, and Littleton and Giles spoke against it, while Heath, who wound up the discussion, is said to have made " a short speech." [166] A bill to continue the session was thereafter sent to the Lords. Then Sir George Moore brought up a report, which produced a debate upon privilege. During this discussion a message

[161] The Lords met at nine on the 7th; see the *Journals,* III, p. 458. Is not Clarendon somewhat inexact, when he says of the Commons (1640): " The house met always at eight of the clock, and rose at twelve; which were the old parliament hours " (I, p. 187)?

[162] I, p. 806.

[163] p. 56.

[164] " A long discourse " he calls it to Carleton; *Fawsley Debates,* p. 153.

[165] *Coke MSS.,* I, p. 209; see Nethersole, writing to Carleton, *F.D.,* p. 155.

[166] *Fawsley Debates,* p. 59.

came down from the Lords that the King " hath appointed to receive the petition from both Houses, this day, at three of the clock, at Hampton Court." But how near was it then to that hour, if we go by what Eliot says? Would the message have been so belated? [167]

(8) The report of the meeting itself would, I fancy, cast grave doubts upon it. For have we not Eliot pleading " the acceptation that was made of the two subsidies which were passed and the satisfaction then professed " by the King and " a larger superstructure " built on it? According to all the authorities, the King expressed no satisfaction in his message of July the 4th. Four versions exist of that message; not one even mentions the grant.[168] But if Charles had " professed satisfaction," it seems to me almost incredible that *all* the reports would ignore it. Moreover, according to Gardiner, " The report in the *Eliot Notes,* in the possession of the Earl of St Germans, like that in the *Fawsley Debates,* is silent on any word in the message about accepting the subsidies." [169] If Charles professed no satisfaction, what becomes of " the larger superstructure " that Eliot builds on the message and thus of the whole alleged meeting?

(9) And what, too, is Buckingham's answer? " That the acceptation which was made of the subsidies then granted was but in respect of the affection to the King, not for satisfaction to his business." There could have been no " acceptation," if nothing was said of the grant. Why, again, did the Duke not retort by denying his visitor's premises? *He* must have known very well what the King said on July the 4th.

(10) Then, if Eliot's tale is reliable, his language is careless and loose. " A new motion," he says, " of supply." Strictly speaking, Coke made no such motion. He asked for no vote of supply. " A present resolution for money is not," he said plainly, " expected."

(11) I confess I feel certain suspicions concerning May's

---

[167] *Commons' Journals,* I, p. 806; *Fawsley Debates,* p. 59.

[168] See the Appendix, p. 174, *infra.*

[169] *History,* V, p. 348, note 3. " Three separate reports of the message " should, properly speaking, be " four."

part in the matter. Would the Chancellor of the Duchy of Lancaster attempt to hold up the King's business?

When these points are all taken together in their cumulative weight and importance, no reliance, I think, can be placed upon Eliot's account of this meeting. It seems at the best very doubtful that any such meeting took place. But some critics will probably ask: "Would Sir John have invented the story?" To this we may venture to answer that he who invented those vetoes would hardly stop short of a meeting. Indeed, when we read of those vetoes, they look like deliberate lying. An Eliot could outdo a Williams in "making relations of things."

CHAPTER IV

THE PARLIAMENT OF 1625 AT OXFORD

THE PLAGUE

Now we come to the sittings at Oxford. To deal with them all day by day would demand by itself a small volume. Nor is it required for our purpose. We long ago raised the main question, "Which side was it opened hostilities? Which declared war on the other?" The answer was given at London before reassembly at Oxford. War was declared by the Commons. June the 30th and July the 5th marked the first great assaults on the Crown. Thus the Oxford debates, on the whole, have a secondary importance and interest. They carry hostilities further; but no one can very well claim that, at least on the main point at issue, we gain from them much further light. Though supply was the principal topic—or shall we say principal pretext?—the Commons showed no disposition at any time during the sittings to perform their own plain obligations. But first a few words of the plague. There is no valid reason for doubting that Oxford was free from the plague, when the parliament broke up in London. We have Charles's word on that point: " I therefore adjourned you to this place, a place then free of that infection, which since it hath pleased God to visit also " ; again, " he made choice of that place, being then the freest of all others from the danger of that grievous sickness." [1] What reason to doubt the King's word? He had shown, indeed, every concern for the safety and protection of his people. He showed some concern for himself. He removed from both Whitehall and Hampton, as soon as the plague appeared there.[2] And, if Oxford was really " the place then freest of all others from the danger of that grievous sickness," then

---

[1] *Lords' Journals*, III, p. 470 ; Rushworth, p. 408 ; *Bibliotheca Regia*, p. 359.
[2] Locke to Carleton, July 9, *Fawsley Debates*, p. 152.

nowhere, it seems, would the Houses be so free from the chance of infection. But the plague at last made its appearance sometime in the end of July. On the 27th day of that month the Vice-Chancellor was writing to Pembroke—the first intimation, it seems, to reach either the King or his ministers.[3] Charles at that time was at Richmond but left on the following day and set out on his journey to Woodstock.[4] No doubt, it would then be too late to arrange for a further adjournment. As yet, too, the danger was slight, for at that time two only had died, though All Souls was described as " shut up." [5] Then again, upon August the 5th we find Whistler reported as stating that only six persons had died, while the sick were but seven or eight only. Three parishes only were infected, although there were thirteen in all.[6] And as Whistler was member for Oxford, he must have known how matters stood. Nor, again, could he well have been tempted to minimize any real danger. We may, I think, fairly conclude that the city was free from the plague, when the Houses adjourned at Westminster. And as for the sojourn at Oxford, no member died there of the plague, though a servant of Beecher's fell a victim.[7]

> He that hath Oxford seen, for beauty, grace,
> And healthiness ne'er saw a better place.

So, indeed, did old Dan Rogers write, that was Clerk to Elizabeth's Council.

Forster, in spite of all this, writes as follows of the London adjournment: " Most special reasons were there also why Oxford should not have been chosen, for already the disease had actually shown itself there." And then in a footnote he adds: " Williams, than whom none is more likely to have known the truth, expressly told Buckingham that two colleges in the university and eight houses in the city had already been visited by the plague. *Scrinia Reserata*, ii. 14." [8]   But

[3] *S.P.D.*, 1625, 1626, p. 74.
[4] Locke to Carleton, August 14 ; *S.P.D.*, p. 84.
[5] See note 3, *supra*.
[6] *Fawsley Debates*, p. 77.
[7] *Ibid.*, p. 151.
[8] *Sir John Eliot*, I, p. 312.

the Lord Keeper told him *at Oxford,* according to my copy
of Hacket, in which it comes two pages later. I cannot
refrain here from adding what Eliot says of the adjournment:
" To sharpen that humour and dislike, at that time happened
also the infection of that place. It was entered into some few
houses of the town, and some of the colleges were infected.
Most of the scholars were retired, and that was an aggravation
to the danger; which being apprehended to the full, became
an aggravation of the fear, by which that fact (though a
justice in the K[ing]) was thought an injury in his servants.
But obedience was resolved on, and through all the difficulties
of the time, the King's pleasure was preferred." [9] Such statements, I think, need no comment beyond that they prove
once again that no faith can be placed in their author.

THE KING IN CHRIST CHURCH HALL

The Commons' House met on the 1st, " very late in the
forenoon," we read, and, moreover, "not many in number." [10]
They decided in London that the House should be " called "
on the fourth sitting day. There were many still on the great
roads, coming up from all parts of the kingdom, as fast as
their coaches allowed. Little business of moment was done,
though some hard words were used of a pardon lately granted
a Jesuit at Exeter. Montague took up the Tuesday; the
third day was " spent in devotion." However, on Thursday,
the 4th—it was then about nine in the morning—the King
came from Woodstock to Oxford, having summoned both
Houses to Christ Church. He came, so says Nethersole,
" privately," meaning, he adds, " without state and usual
solemnity at his entry into towns "—no doubt, on account of
the plague. [11] Coke arrived on the Tuesday in Oxford and had
his instructions that evening to speak to the lower house only.
But these were the next evening cancelled and all, as he tells
us, " left doubtful." What was the line to be taken? Should
Conway or Coke state the case in the presence of Charles to

[9] *Negotium Posterorum,* I, p. 124.
[10] *Fawsley Debates,* p. 68.
[11] *Ibid.,* p. 154.

both Houses? These questions, indeed, were not settled, when Charles reached the Hall in the morning, for " counsel " there " varied again." Then the King's resolution was taken—" to show the importance of the fleet," which, however, could not put to sea unless further supply was forthcoming in the nature of " money or credit." Charles himself would " deliver his mind," to be followed by Conway and Coke, the former " required to say something," the latter " presenting the rest." So the King first addressed the two Houses in a speech so " effectual " and " clear " that Coke thought it would weigh with them more than could anything said by his ministers.[12] Let us again hear the King, who was once more both brief and concise :

" My Lords, and you of the Commons, well all remember, that, from your desires and advice, my father (now with God) brake off those two treaties with Spain that were then in hand ; well you then foresaw, that, as well for regaining my dispossessed brother's inheritance, as home defence, a war was likely to succeed ; and that, as your counsels had led my father into it, so your assistances in a Parliamentary way to pursue it should not be wanting. The aid you gave him, by advice, was for succour of his allies, guarding Ireland, and the home parts, supply of munition, preparing and setting forth of his navy. A Council you thought on and appointed for the war, and Treasurers for issuing of your monies. And, to begin this work of your advice, you gave three subsidies, and as many fifteens, which with speed were levied, and by direction of that Council of War (in which the preparation of this navy was not the least) disbursed. It pleased God, at the entrance of this preparation (by your advice begun), to call my father to His mercy ; whereby I entered as well to the care of your designs, as his Crown. I did not then, as princes of custom do, and for formality, reassemble you ; but that, by your further advice and aid, I might be able to proceed in that, which, by your counsels, my father was now engaged

<hr />

[12] See the long and important letter from Coke to Lord Brooke on the 4th ; *Coke MSS.*, I, p. 208. I presume that " the Hall where we met " is no other than the hall of Christ Church.

in. Your love to me, and forwardness to further those affairs, you expressed by a grant of two subsidies, yet ungathered; although I must assure you, by myself and others, upon credit taken up, and aforehand disbursed; all far too short as yet to set forth that navy now preparing, as I have lately found by estimate of those of care and skill employed about it. Before you could be acquainted fully with those necessities of further aid, it pleased God to visit the place of your assembly then with a grievous plague. To stay you in that danger, had been a neglect of my just care. To prorogue the Parliament, had destroyed the enterprise. I therefore adjourned you to this place, a place then free of that infection, which since it hath pleased God to visit also. Here then to hold you long, against your own desires, were to express in me little care of your safeties; and to adjourn it without your further helps, were to destroy the preparations already made. I therefore leave the care of both to your elections, resolutions, and answers; only acquainting you with my own opinion, which is, that better far it were both for your honours and mine, that with hazard of half the fleet, it were set forth, than with assured loss of so much provision stayed at home.

" When you shall be pleased, of the whole particular of all expenses about this preparation to take an account, my Lord Treasurer there, and other the Ministers employed, shall acquaint you." [13]

From this speech, as it stands in the *Journals,* it seems that, entirely or mainly, the King was concerned for *the fleet.* It was aid for the fleet that he sought. This is fully confirmed by Coke's letter, on which I have already drawn. Let me cite here the relevant words. " But the resolution upon the present, which the King himself delivered to me in his chair was to show the importance of the Fleet, and that it could not proceed without a present supply by money or credit, which is the business which now possesseth and troubleth the whole House : and to-morrow morning is appointed to begin to debate it. The King himself first

---

[13] *Lords' Journals,* III, p. 470. Rushworth (p. 177) omits a good part of the speech.

delivered his mind effectually and clearly to this end, and I presume that will be of more force to sway our resolution than anything that could be said by any of his servants." [14] Nothing, indeed, could be plainer. This passage may very well lead us to doubt that the *Journals* themselves give an adequate report of the King. There are, indeed, other good reasons for thinking the reports in the *Journals* do not do his speeches full justice. Coke's statements themselves are confirmed by a further report of the speech. " And on the fourth day, which was Thursday, both houses were appointed to meet in Christ Church hall at 9 o'clock before his Majesty ; where he first himself speak unto them, showing them his wants, and the great necessity he had of money to set out this fleet ; which could not be done without their supply." [15] This reporter—a member of parliament—grasped the main point of the speech.

Charles was followed by Conway and Coke, described in the margin of the *Journals* as " Secretaries of State " ; but Coke was a Master of Requests, Albert Morton, though abroad on a mission, still alive at that time and in office.[16] If we follow the *Fawsley Debates,* Conway " recited the difference betwixt the state of affairs now and when the late King began first to think upon arms." At the same time, the fleet, as I think, is the main point in Conway's oration. " The fleet hath cost a great mass ; there wants more, without which it cannot go to sea, and, if it should so fall out, it will discourage those Princes. The time of the year is almost past, the officers are discredited by reason of the infection, all that you gave last is employed. They are disappointed of 30 or 40,000 pounds at this instant." And Conway concluded as follows : " The honour and safety of this nation and religion are at the stake : if we now grow cold, the Princes of Germany will divide, the King of France come in as a party to the Catholic league ; the King of Denmark make his peace

---

[14] See p. 85, n. 12, *supra.*
[15] *Harl. MSS.* 5007, fol. 75, reproduced in the *Fawsley Debates,* p. 129.
[16] *Lords' Journals,* III, p. 471. While claiming to give both the speeches or, at least, the " effect " of both speeches, they seem to give that by Coke only.

with the Emperor; which difficulties his Majesty, finding an impossibility in himself to remove, hath resorted to the help of his subject, which his ancestors have always found ready in the like cases." [17]

Then Coke was " called up to the King " and, receiving some private instructions, " returned to the middle of the hall," whence he made a speech " near an hour long," much resembling his speech in July.[18]   But his main point was also the fleet, and upon it, like Conway, he ended. " The fleet is now at the sea going to the rendezvous at Plymouth, where there lie 10,000 men at pay, for which action his Majesty is deeply engaged in respect of his own honour, the cause of religion, and support of his allies. He hath intelligence besides of a purpose to trouble Ireland, to increase the enemy['s] army in the Low Countries, and to thrust over part of [his] army hither. There is no less disbursed already than 400,000 pounds; his Majesty's coffers are empty.[19] It is fit you should consider what to do. No King loves his subjects, the laws and religion, better than he, and he is persuaded no subjects love their Prince better; therefore, he leaves it to your choice what to do, so as it may be put into the balance whether it is better to suffer this action to fall, or to stay awhile together that you may resolve to yield him convenient help." [20] So it was for the fleet—the fleet only— that Charles, Coke and Conway were pleading. If Conway and Coke spoke at large, not confining their remarks to the navy, we need, I think, feel no surprise. For the navy was merely a means to promoting a definite policy—a policy Charles from the first was resolved to make clear to both Houses. The navy, too, brooked no delay. But the King could have asked for much more from a parliament pledged to the hilt. There were several could not hear the speeches,

---

[17] *Fawsley Debates*, pp. 73, 74.

[18] *Ibid.*, pp. 74ff.; *Coke MSS.*, I, p. 209; Nethersole to Carleton, *Fawsley Debates*, p. 155.

[19] Notice this very plain statement.

[20] *Fawsley Debates*, p. 76. This is fully confirmed by the following: " And then also spoke Sir John Cooke, by the King's appointment, of the preparation of the Navy, and of the charge of it." The writer again grasps the point. See p. 87, n. 15, *supra*.

and so the King's cause may have suffered. Sir John Davers asked the next morning to have the heads set down on paper; but this was refused or ignored.[21]

To conclude with some words on a point which, perhaps, deserves mention in passing. "It was felt," Gardiner tells us of Coke, "as a mark of disrespect that they should be addressed in the King's name by a man who was not a minister of state."[22] The writer by "they" means the Commons. But what does Coke say of himself? "The envy that I bear is that it hath not been known nor is agreeable to the orders of the House (as some think) that a nether house man was ever employed to deliver the King's pleasure to both Houses of Parliament, which came to pass at this time only by reason of the sudden change of counsel which gave not time to any other to be instructed for a speech of near an hour long."[23] Gardiner could hardly have seen the long letter from which I am quoting. It explains, I think, Phelips's words on the following day in the House. Meaning Coke, he referred to "a gentleman, who did that yesterday which never any man did before."[24] When Buckingham addressed the two Houses in Christ Church on August the 8th, Charles, remembering all this about Coke, asked the Commons to allow him to speak.[25] But how hard were the Commons to please! Had an "upper-house" man and no other addressed them by command of the King and so "moved," as it were, "for a subsidy," what would such sticklers have said? And how bitter were Phelips and others, how lacking in all sense of humour!

SUPPLY REQUIRED FOR THE FLEET

And now let us come to the figures. "They are disappointed of 30 or 40,000 pounds at this instant." The words "at this instant" are important. "There is no less disbursed already than 400,000 pounds." This, I think, should be

[21] Fawsley Debates, p. 77.
[22] History, V, p. 406.
[23] Coke MSS., I, p. 209.
[24] Fawsley Debates, p. 80.
[25] See Commons' Journals, I, p. 812.

three hundred thousand. " Disbursed " means " disbursed on the fleet." Buckingham informed the two Houses at Christ Church on August the 8th : " 2. The second question : Whether those expenses, computed for this business, of 400,000 pounds, whereof 300,000 pounds already disbursed, 40,000 pounds are presently to be used, and 60,000 pounds at the return, have been bestowed in that frugal manner as is fit or no? All was managed by the proper officers : I laid out money of my own, and borrowed of my friends, but I made it to run the proper way, as if it had come out of the Excheq[ue]r. Here Sir John Cooke said :—Your own 44,000 pounds, and another particular purse, 50,000 pounds. 3. The third question : Whether yet there be a considerable sum wanting to set out the fleet, without which it cannot go to the sea, and whether this fleet was ever intended to go forth or not. To set out this fleet 40,000 pounds is wanting. My master hath anticipated all his revenue, pawned his lands, and would have pawned his plate, if it would have been accepted, so that his Majesty must live in misery unless some course be taken for his supply. For the second part of the question : Whether it were intended the fleet should go forth or no? For my part I know not what policy my master should have, to set out a fleet with the charge of 400,000 pounds only to abuse the world, and lessen his people, and to put you to such hazard. What should my master gain? Would he do an act never to meet with you again? Certainly he would never have employed so great a sum of money, but that he saw the necessity of the affairs of Christendom require it ; and it was done with an intention to set it out with all the speed that may be." [26] The Lord Treasurer, Ley, also stated : " The furnishing of the navy 300,000 pounds, and [100,000] pounds is wanting, whereof 40,000 pounds presently, and 60,000 pounds at their return." [27] These statements appear to

[26] *Fawsley Debates,* p. 98 ; *Lords' Journals,* III, p. 482. The latter have this absurd note : " This vast sum of forty thousand pounds, bestowed upon the Navy."

[27] *Fawsley Debates,* p. 104. See *Lords' Journals,* III, p. 484 : " The Navy, three hundred thousand pounds, and one hundred thousand pounds to be disbursed : *videlicet,* forty thousand pounds now, and sixty thousand pounds at the return."

agree. We may, therefore, draw certain conclusions. The
forty thousand pounds Conway mentioned were only a part
of the money required at that time for the fleet. Sixty
thousand would also be wanted—no doubt, for the payment
of wages [28]—or one hundred thousand in all. Then some
ninety-four thousand were borrowed or actually lent by the
Duke, or a total in all for the fleet of one hundred and ninety-
four thousand.[29]

Now turn to the debate of the 5th. There we find that
both Edmondes and Weston propounded a definite motion,
according to the *Fawsley Debates*. " Two subsidies and two
fifteens " was the grant they proposed in the House, " for
that less," so the latter observed, " will not serve for the
present occasion." The *Journals* themselves credit Heath with
precisely the same proposition, " two subsidies, two fifteens,
payable in October and April come-twelve-month," though
we read in the *Fawsley Debates* he " concluded that it was
fit to give; and for the *quantum* did refer it to a second
question." [30] Why were all three agreed on this figure? For
no one, I think, can suppose that they hit on it simply at
random. I suggest that the true explanation is really contained in those statements with which I have just now been
dealing. Two subsidies, two fifteens, came, in rough and
approximate figures, to two hundred thousand pounds. But
that was, as nearly as may be, the total required for the fleet.
And it follows, if this is correct, that the vote then proposed
in the Commons was intended entirely for the fleet. I may
add that this explanation agrees with Coke's letter to Brooke.
Were it said, " the full needs of the navy had not been made
known to the Commons until Buckingham spoke on the 8th,"
I should answer that this was not so. I assume here, for
argument's sake, that the King did not go into figures. But

---

[28] " 60,000 pounds to pay wages when they come home "; Seymour on
August 11 in Appendix to *Fawsley Debates*, p. 146.

[29] I do not include the King's loan, which amounted to twenty thousand
pounds, called by Weston " his debt for this action." But, whether
included or not, such a sum leaves my points unaffected.

[30] *Fawsley Debates*, pp. 80, 84; *Commons' Journals*, I, p. 810. But
the *Journals* are not of much use. They apparently, indeed, credit
Seymour with moving the very same sum!

the deficit due to the loans Coke had stated on July the 8th. "The King, when Prince, took up for the Navy; the Duke, above 44,000 pounds, other Officers of State, for about 50,000 pounds." And "shall it be said," Coke remarked, "that these men are left to be undone by their readiness to public services?" [31] These figures Coke may have repeated in his speech upon August the 4th; he repeated, no doubt, a good deal.[32] With regard to the forty thousand pounds there can hardly be any dispute, though, to go by the *Lord's Journals* only, that sum was not mentioned on the 4th.[33] This leaves but the sixty thousand. In the speeches of Conway and Coke in the *Fawsley Debates* and the *Journals,* it is true, no such figure is mentioned. But nothing, indeed, is more likely than that Conway, who mentioned the smaller, would mention the larger sum also. May or Edmondes, if not Coke or Conway, I think, must have certainly done so. How else should we find Phelips saying, when he spoke on the 5th after Edmondes: "It seems strange it should be so hard for the King to take up 60,000 pounds; God forgive them that have so decayed his credit." [34] What else could the speaker allude to? A statement's not being reported, I think I need hardly remark, is no proof of its not being made. Other things not reported were mentioned—or, at least, we may fairly suppose so. For instance, Strode knew on the 6th that the fleet was to go in a fortnight.[35] There is nothing of Edmondes's speech, as distinct from the motion he made, in the *Fawsley Debates* or the *Journals,* but in the appendix to the former we are told he "began the motion to give this day, showed his Majesty's wants, our engagements, and the dishonour that would ensue to the King and kingdom by relapse, and so moveth to give two subsidies "—inserted, it seems, as an afterthought.[36]

[31] *Commons' Journals,* I, p. 806; *Fawsley Debates,* p. 58.
[32] See p. 88, *supra,* and note.
[33] See *Lords' Journals,* III, p. 471.
[34] *Fawsley Debates,* p. 82.
[35] *Ibid.,* p. 90. "How can two subsidies to be paid a year hence conduce to the going out of the navy within this fortnight?" To this we can, no doubt, reply that the sum would be taken on credit or, if not the whole, then so much as was there and then actually needed.
[36] *Ibid.,* p. 135.

The King and his ministers, therefore, confined their demands to the fleet, *though they well might have asked for much more and the Commons were "engaged" more extensively.* Charles thus no longer called on them to honour the rest of their pledges. The subsidies previously voted were likewise assigned to the fleet. This seems clear from the following statements. "Your love to me," Charles told the Houses, "and forwardness to further those affairs, you expressed by a grant of two subsidies, yet ungathered; although I must assure you, by myself and others, upon credit taken up, and aforehand disbursed; all far too short as yet to set forth that navy now preparing, as I have lately found by estimate of those of care and skill employed about it." [37] Coke had stated on July the 8th: "The charges of this fleet, only in the office of the navy, is above 20,000. In the office of the ordinance 48,000; for the land men will be 45,000 pounds; whereof the two subsidies which are now given will amount but to 160,000." [38] So Conway had said, as we saw: "The time of the year is almost past, the officers are discredited by reason of the infection, all that you gave last is employed." [39] Thus all that was voted in London or might now be voted in Oxford had gone or would go to the fleet. If Conway and Coke spoke at length of the policy adopted by the King, then their statements were, no doubt, intended, in part, to inform the two Houses, in part, to show Charles's inability, at least by any ordinary methods, to raise any further supplies. What, again, shall we say of this point? May on August the 5th moved "to give, in respect of the pressing necessity, which is, that this great design of the fleet must stay unless it be supplied by us; and withal showed, that if money could have been taken up to set out this fleet upon his Majesty's plate, jewels, and some of his Lords', we had not been called together now." [40] In other words, but for the fleet there had

---

[37] See p. 86, *supra.*
[38] *Fawsley Debates,* p. 57.
[39] See p. 87, *supra.*
[40] *Fawsley Debates,* p. 135. See Weston on August the 10th: "If land, plate, or jewels could have [procured] it, we had not now been troubled." This he said of the forty thousand pounds. See *F.D.,* p. 112.

not been a session at Oxford. And so there had, *a fortiori,* been no propositions for money.

My account is, moreover, consistent with the message delivered by Weston to the Commons on August the 10th. I shall quote from the *Fawsley Debates:* "His Majesty hath taken knowledge of your desire to reform many things tending to his particular service, and is well pleased with this your intention "—how he keeps even now his good temper, still making so gracious an answer!—" but desireth you to take consideration of these points : that this time is fit only for such matters as are of present necessity and dispatch; that the fleet stays for your resolution, and the season of the year is near spent, though the opportunity be not yet past; that, if the plague should fall into the navy or army, all the action is lost, and if it should fall among yourselves, which God forbid, it will breed much danger and distraction, which his Majesty is loath to think upon. His desire is that you will presently resolve whether, upon the important reasons delivered unto us, so much importing his honour, you will supply his necessity in such a proportion that he may send his navy; otherwise, if this will not move you, his Majesty will take more care of your safety than your selves, because the sickness disperseth in this town, and he will do all as well as he may in such as extremity, wherein he may so much suffer. But if you will give a present dispatch of the supply, he doth promise, in the word of a King, giving you that royal word which he had never yet broken, nor given cause to mistrust, that you shall meet again in the winter in a more seasonable time, and stay together till you may bring to maturity those things which were propounded; and that his Majesty will then do whatsoever belongs to a good and gracious King. This is his message, and he desires you withal to remember that it is the first request that ever he made to you." [41] Again, let us note " all the action." From beginning to end of the session the King is concerned with " this action."

This brings us to one further point. For Coke's speech upon August the 4th does in one respect differ, I think, from

[41] *Fawsley Debates,* p. 106.

the speech that he made in July. While in August he spoke of " this action," he spoke in July in the plural. He then said " these things " or " these actions." " By money or credit " alone could " these things," as he then said, " subsist "; he was anxious for the House at that time " to declare our forwardness to supply the actions now begun." The naval operations were vital : " The King, when he was Prince, borrowed 20,000 pounds for these provisions, my L[ord] Admiral hath engaged all his estate, other ministers have furnished above 50,000 pounds. Shall it be said that these men are left to be undone by their readiness to public services ? Shall we proclaim our own poverty by losing all that is bestowed upon the enterprise, because we cannot go through with it ? What shall we say to the honour of the King ? But this is not all : even the establishment of his Majesty in his royal throne, the peace of Christendom, the state of religion, depends upon this fleet." But it certainly seems from the con-text that assistance for Christian and Mansfeld came under the head of " these actions." [42]

Provided my view is correct, the remarks Gardiner makes in his *History* appear to be wide of the point. I cannot go into them fully; suffice it to quote some examples. " Charles had dwelt entirely on the fleet. Conway, who followed, took a wider view of the situation. Having said that 30,000*l*. or 40,000*l*. were wanted to enable the fleet to start, he afterwards drew a picture in the background of the Continent in flames, and hinted at the large sums needed for keeping the Protestant forces on foot in Germany and the Netherlands. There was thus a discrepancy between the smallness of the sum named and the largeness of the expenditure hinted at. To fulfil his engagements, Charles wanted not 40,000*l*. but some 7,000,000*l*. or 8,000,000*l*. at the least. To make up his mind to forego this and to be content with the smaller sum would probably have been his wisest course, and if he had adopted it he might perhaps have avoided summoning Parliament at all. This, however, was precisely what he was unable to bring his mind to. He, therefore, it may be supposed, whilst

[42] *Fawsley Debates,* pp. 58, 59.

authorizing Conway to mention the fact that no more than 30,000*l*. or 40,000*l*. was needed for the fleet, allowed his greater expenses to be expounded in the hope of stirring the liberality of the Commons to the utmost." [43] So, also, we find in a footnote : " Eliot, as is well known, believed that Buckingham wanted to be denied. I am quite unable to take this view of the case after a full consideration of Buckingham's whole proceedings, of which an historian is now able to know much of which Eliot knew nothing. It is likely enough, as I have before said, that he expected to be denied, and that he intended to make use of the impression caused by his being in the right and the Commons in the wrong, when success came. Nor can I see that he only asked for 40,000*l*. at first. I fancy he simply wanted that at least, and would take as much more as he could get—a frame of mind the very opposite to that of Gustavus, who at once refused to engage in war except on his own terms." [44] All this is the purest conjecture with not a real fact to support it. And Buckingham now is the villain, which comes, I presume, of relying on Eliot's mischievous tract. But suppose the Duke now *was* the villain. Why he (or the King, for that matter) should ask for so small a supply as two subsidies, two fifteens, and, moreover, should hit on that sum passes all understanding, I think. For a man who, according to Gardiner, expected the House would " deny " him, although he would take all he could, had lost nothing by asking for more. The more that he asked, on the contrary, the greater the chance, he would argue, that *something*, at least, would be voted. Again, " Coke's hearers were thus left in uncertainty, an uncertainty which was doubtless shared by the King himself, how much they were really expected to grant. The small sum needed for the fleet was fixed and definite. All else was hazy and impalpable. The success of the fleet might perhaps enable Charles to dispense with the supplies which he needed for other purposes. His error was that he did not come forward, as Gustavus had come forward in the negotiations of the past winter, with a

[43] *History*, V, p. 404.
[44] V, p. 408, n. 1.

definite demand which he himself recognized as indispensable. He tried to influence the minds of the members without first making up his own." [45] One comment seems very unjust: "It needed the utmost frankness of explanation on the part of the ministers of Charles to do away with the ill-will caused by the long reticence of the King, followed by the involved and almost unintelligible demands which had been made at the close of the sittings of Westminster, and which were now repeated at Oxford in a form more involved and unintelligible still." [46] "The ill-will caused by the long reticence of the King"—we have seen from what the Commons did in London how baseless was that taunt, at least. After this we are hardly surprised to find Gardiner remarking as follows: "Nor did Edmondes, who followed, mend the position of the Government by asking directly for two subsidies and two fifteenths, about 200,000*l.*, a sum far too great for supplying the immediate needs of the fleet, whilst altogether inadequate to meet Charles's engagements on the Continent." [47] Gardiner, it seems to me clear, has entirely misread the whole matter. So lame a conclusion, indeed, should itself suggest further inquiry. "Involved," "unintelligible" and so on the statements are certainly not, even judged by the records surviving. I claim to have made this much clear.

EVASION

I propose to deal briefly with the Commons. I said there was no inclination at any time during the sittings to fulfil their own plain obligations. Whoever will study the proceedings will, I think, bear me out in that verdict. They refused further aid for the fleet, though the fleet, at least, brooked no delay. There was nought they would not do but give. They would roam over tonnage and poundage and argue about "impositions," "make this parliament the reformer of the Commonwealth"—ominous word, that word "Commonwealth"!— "do somewhat to make" the King "glorious," examine and

[45] V, p. 405.
[46] V, p. 406.
[47] V, p. 408.

reform the King's revenue, hunt down the priests and the Jesuits. These and other topics they broached, while ostensibly debating supply.[48] They professed their annoyance with the summons, complaining that the plague was in Oxford. Seymour " knew no ground of this meeting unless some out of private ends seek to put dissension betwixt the King and his people, and gave this advice out of ignorance or malice, rather than out of any care of the Commonwealth "—a veiled but clear hint at the Duke.[49] And Phelips the same day declared, " he was against the opinion of those that would part, and doubted not but God had brought us hither against reason and precedent, that we may do somewhat to make his Majesty glorious." [50] And so it was providence really, not some " out of ignorance or malice." Then, again, when dissolution was imminent, Sir Robert More, supported by others, " moved that we should send some humble message to his Majesty desiring longer respite, both for his business and the Commonwealth's." Phelips objected to the motion but only, as it seems, on the ground " that rumours were no warrant for our belief, nor for such a message. We ought to go on in our business, and when we receive any such notice of the King's pleasure, to obey it." [51]

The Commons' " engagements " were touched on—but seldom and only in passing. On these there was no unanimity. Clearly these men were uneasy, for some would deny them *in toto* and others explain them away. Sir E. Coke observed, for example : " I. That we had engaged the King. *Ans.* We made a protestation, which is a parliamentary way ; but there [is] no enemy yet known. Our country doth not trust us to engage them but only by Act of Parliament, and yet, if we were engaged, we have performed it ; we gave the last Parliament 400,000 pounds, now two subsidies, besides the

---

[48] See *Fawsley Debates* and appendix, *passim*.
[49] *Fawsley Debates*, p. 78.
[50] *Ibid.*, p. 80. " Concluding," wrote Nethersole of Phelips, " that by all means since we were here we should resolve to sit it out notwithstanding the danger of the plague " (to Carleton on August the 9th ; F.D., p. 156).
[51] *Ibid.*, p. 124.

tonnage and poundage." No enemy known, but they gave! And Phelips had just before argued that "since that King's death, there is a wrong done to us in levying the tonnage and poundage"! [52] Coke, at least, might have stuck to his facts. Then, according to Whistler, "There can be no engagement. If there were, yet is there no honesty to perform it when it concerns the country that we should not." [53] The Commons themselves were to judge when their own plighted word might be broken. Yet Eliot admitted the engagement; he merely denied the necessity. "The supply demanded is grounded upon a double argument—promise, and reason; promise, that we are engaged; and he conceiveth that we are engaged; but he doth not think that there is such a necessity as is pretended." [54] Alford, it seems, went with Coke, but he made the same point more explicitly: "He holdeth we are not engaged to give for the recovery of the Palatinate; for when it was in the Act of Parliament, as it was first penned, it was strucken out by the order of the House, as a thing unfit to engage the House for the recovery of the Palatinate; and if possible, yet not without great charge and difficulty; and not to give now; but to make unto the King an humble remonstrance of our reasons why we do not give at this time," or, again, as the shorter version has it, "That [it] was never the meaning of the House to be engaged; therefore all words which might receive any such interpretation were stricken out of the preamble of the Act, and we ought now to be as careful to grant subsidies in reversion." [55] Gardiner writes thus of this speech: "The full truth was out at last. The House did not mean to support Mansfeld and the King of Denmark, and Buckingham and the King would have to reconcile themselves to the fact." [56] As between the two Houses and the King it is clear that the Act was irrelevant. The Commons were "engaged" by their address; they could not shift their ground in the Act and then treat the address as non-existent.

[52] *Ibid.*, pp. 84, 81.
[53] *Ibid.*, p. 122.
[54] *Ibid.*, p. 137.
[55] *Fawsley Debates*, pp. 135, 88.
[56] *History*, V, p. 412.

But, even had Alford been right, his contention was no less irrelevant. Supply was desired for the fleet, not at all for continental alliances. No doubt, that address was inconvenient. So far as, at least, I can gather, not one of the opposition leaders referred to it under its name. Yet Buckingham based his case on it, when he spoke upon August the 8th,[57] as did Nethersole, too, on the 5th: " King James was engaged to the King and Q[ueen] of Bohemia : he took the way of treaty to fulfil that engagement. That treaty, though it could not restore all the Palatinate, yet a great part was offered. The King's resolution to leave that course was upon our promise to assist him in a Parliamentary way." [58] Said Naunton, again, on the 10th : " The reputation of the King and kingdom, and of this House, being all engaged, if not by law, yet by a public declaration of our intentions." [59]

The Commons, I think, in plain language, cared nothing about their own pledges and were utterly dishonest and unscrupulous, converting an answer on supply into one great assault on the Duke. Their intention was clear from the outset. Historians for once are agreed, and I feel myself, therefore, absolved from adducing—or repeating—the evidence. I think it sufficient to add that, though Eliot declared on the 6th, " I dare, in my conscience, clear and vindicate that noble Lord who hath had some aspersions laid upon him ; and that if there hath been any abuse in the fleet it is not his fault, for there is a commission for the furnishing of this Navy, which is no new thing " [60] (a reflection, of course, upon others, that Coke, at least, strongly resented), the mask was thrown off five days later, when we come to these plain words by Seymour : " Let us lay the fault where it is ; the Duke of Buckingham is trusted, and it must needs be either in him or his agents." [61] Indeed, I conceive that the Duke was attacked

[57] *Fawsley Debates*, p. 96 ; *Lords' Journals*, III, p. 482. In the latter we find the address is described as " the Act of both Houses."
[58] *Fawsley Debates*, p. 89.
[59] *Ibid.*, p. 107. Naunton was Master of the Wards.
[60] *Ibid.*, p. 138.
[61] *Ibid.*, p. 118 ; *Commons' Journals*, I, p. 815. " The Lord Admiral hath the care of these things : therefore the default must needs be in him, or his agents."

at some earlier stage and attacked in plain terms and by name. For if not, why should Eliot have said, " But I dare, in my conscience, clear and vindicate that noble Lord who hath had some aspersions laid upon him," while Clarke on the same morning said " that some of this house did use some particularities with bitter invectives, not fit for this time, and that against the greatest officer of state in this kingdom; which he for his part, as being advanced by him, was bound to oppose " ? [62]   The next step to attacking the Duke was attacking his master directly.

We may add just a word on one point, which, although it is quite incidental, yet throws a strange light on the men who refused the King aid for the fleet.   Sir E. Coke, opposed to supply, yet declared on the 10th in the House that " for his own part he would give a thousand pounds as a private man, not as a Parliament man; and that willingly, notwithstanding all his crosses, and hoped those of the King's council would do as much."   Yet his friends had declared the plan faulty or held that no money was needed or Charles could take money on credit.   Mansell, who spoke after Coke, was opposed to the plan for the fleet but would give, he said, two hundred pounds.[63]   Let them have a benevolence, therefore, and sink their own wealth in the sea !   Coke's expressing a hope that the ministers might do as much as he would must have sounded like some sorry jest.   Had not Buckingham borrowed and lent on a far greater scale to the state with, it seemed, little hope of recovery?

GLANVILLE'S PROTESTATION : THE WARFARE
OF WORDS

In conclusion, it is not without interest to note what took place on the 12th in the very last hours of the session.   The House was again in committee to consider the question of " giving."   " It was moved," say the *Fawsley Debates,* " we should fall to draw reasons of our refusal: opposed by Sir Rob[er]t More as not seasonable, because we had not yet

[62] *Fawsley Debates,* p. 139.
[63] *Ibid.,* p. 115.

refused. And that we might not refuse, Sir Francis Nethersall pressed the danger of the Imperial Diet to confirm the Bonn." They had not, indeed, formally refused; their intention, however, was evident. Then followed a long speech from Sherland; but what happened next is uncertain. According to the *Fawsley Debates,* " Mr. Alpharde propounded three heads of declaration to the King: 1. thanks for his answer concerning religion; 2. for his care of our healths; 3. a profession of our love and affection to his Majesty. Mr. Glanvill. There are divers ways of declaring ourselves to the King, sometimes by message, by petition, by committees, by entry of some act or protestation amongst ourselves. He doubted we had not time for any of the former, and therefore advised the later way; and to that purpose presented the form of a protestation, ready drawn in these words," etc.[64] The other report omits Alford. Giving Sherland at length, it continues: " Now the house resolved to frame an humble remonstrance to his Majesty; and then news was brought by the Serjeant, that the Usher of the upper house was at door, and had a message to deliver from the Lords; but before they would suffer Mr. Solicitor to depart out of the chair, since they had not time to make a remonstrance to his Majesty, they would make a protestation, expressing their dutiful affection. And thereupon Mr. Glanvile stood up and declared a short protestation which he had framed in writing; which the house approved; and so he was required to go down and stand by the Clerk whiles he read it; which he did; and then it was ordered to be entered: which was to this effect," etc.[65] When the Speaker returned to the chair, " A protestation," we read in the *Journals,* " agreed upon by the Grand Committee, reported to the House by Mr. Solicitor; to be entered into the Clerk's book; and to be presented to his Majesty by all the Privy Council, and Sir J. Fullerton, and Sir Ro. Carre, from the House. This, upon question, allowed, and to be entered, *ut supra;* without one negative voice. Upon a second question, the Privy Council of the

[64] *Fawsley Debates,* pp. 124-5.
[65] *Ibid.,* pp. 148-50.

House, accompanied with Sir J. Fullerton, and Sir Ro. Carre, shall, with all convenient speed, present this to his Majesty, in writing." [66] Then at last was the Usher admitted. And the Commons had commenced the long warfare of protests, declarations, remonstrances. This paper is not in the *Journals* but is given in the *Fawsley Debates*: " We, the Knights, Citizens, and Burgesses of the Commons House of Parliament, being the representative body of the whole Commons of this Realm, abundantly comforted in his Majesty's late gracious answer touching religion, and his message for the care of our healths, do solemnly protest and vow before God and the world, with one heart and voice, that we are all resolved and do hereby declare that we will ever continue most loyal and obedient subjects to our most gracious sovereign King Charles, and that we will be ready in convenient time, and in a Parliamentary way, freely and dutifully to do our uttermost endeavour to discover and reform the abuses and grievances of the Realm and State; and, in the like sort, to afford all necessary supply to his Majesty, upon his present and all other his just occasions and designs; most humbly beseeching our ever dear and dread sovereign, in his princely wisdom and goodness, to rest assured of the true and hearty affections of his poor Commons, and to esteem the same, as we conceive it indeed, the greatest worldly reputation and security a just King can have, and to account all such as slanderers of the people's affections [and?] enemies of the Commonwealth, that shall dare to say the contrary." [67] These proceedings are all of a piece with their conduct since June the 18th. " In convenient time " they will give, but they do not intend to vote money, when money is urgently needed. Who thinks them sincere, let him do so. The King, " our ever dear and dread sovereign, in his princely wisdom and goodness," is " to rest assured of the true and hearty affections of his poor Com-

[66] *Commons' Journals*, I, p. 815.
[67] *Fawsley Debates*, p. 125. The last clause requires the " and." With slight verbal differences only this paper is given by Rushworth *(Historical Recollections*, p. 190) ; by Eliot, too, in his tract *(Negotium Posterorum*, II, p. 105). This instance, with others, goes to show that, when Eliot's tract was composed, he did not rely solely on memory but must have had documents by him.

mons." Was not James "to rest confidently assured, that, if you shall be engaged in a real war, we your loyal and loving subjects will never fail to assist your Majesty, in a parliamentary way"?

"THE PLATFORM OF SIR NATHANIEL RICH"

If nothing has so far been said of the speeches of August the 6th, it comes from my being unable to adopt or to follow the reasoning which Gardiner sets out in the preface prefixed to the *Fawsley Debates* and repeats in his *History* more briefly, and also, in part, from the fact that, whatever the meaning placed on them, they are but additional proof that the Commons at no time were willing to fulfil their own plain obligations.

Let me first quote a few words from Gardiner. He describes the debate in his preface and comments upon it as follows: "What then was the meaning of all this? The speeches of Mildmay, Coryton, Eliot, Strode, and Rich all point in one direction; they all express a willingness to grant supply in one form or another, but all accompany it with more or less stringent conditions. The King, according to Rich, would have to give up his claim to the impositions; Buckingham would have to submit to see his designs criticized by a settled Council. And yet neither Heath, nor Weston, nor any one else on the part of the Government, rose to object." "The move thus made," we are told, may be "fairly regarded as one proceeding from the wiser friends of Buckingham. How far it had already been submitted to his approval is a question of no very material importance." But "that Buckingham had been made aware, on the afternoon of the 5th, of what was to be proposed on the following day" is pronounced a "very probable inference." [68] Then Gardiner remarks in his *History*: "The next morning, after a brisk passage on a protection accorded by Conway to a Roman Catholic lady in Dorsetshire, the great debate was resumed. The course which it took was altogether different

[68] *Fawsley Debates,* p. xvii.

from that of the preceding day. The 5th had been given up
to a conflict between the ministers of the Crown and the men
who, in modern political language, would be termed the
advanced wing of the Opposition. On the 6th all is changed.
Phelips, Coke, and Seymour are as silent as Weston, Heath,
and Edmondes. It looks as if both parties had come to a
tacit agreement to allow a body of mediators to declare the
terms on which an understanding might yet be effected." [69]
In a word, the five men above mentioned attempted a compromise with Buckingham.

How far is all this consistent with what the reports have
to tell us? To mention a few of the points. Did all the five
speakers referred to " express a willingness to grant supply in
one form or another, but all accompany it with more or less
stringent conditions "? And *when* was supply to be voted—
a point of some little importance? Mildmay, so far as I see,
was for voting an *immediate* supply, " by way," as he said,
" of contribution," while asking what sum would be needed.
I find here no " stringent conditions." He considered the
Commons " engaged "—he defined in what sense more
precisely—and nothing would thus be less likely than his
moving supply on conditions.[70] Coryton demanded " a committee to consider of what fit to be done, both for supply of the
King, and relief of the kingdom : wherein religion to have the
first place." [71] Note again this resorting to " religion." His
remarks on supply are ambiguous : " he would have the King
supplied if there be a necessity," but whether he allowed the
necessity we have, I fear, no means of knowing—nor, again,
when supply would be voted, provided his motion was carried.
But we do know that on the 11th he refused to give during
that session.[72] As for Eliot, so far as I see, he desired
prorogation or adjournment. " First to resolve, whether fit
to petition the King for a recess now—moveth, a committee,

[69] *History*, V, p. 412.
[70] *Commons' Journals*, I, p. 811 ; *Fawsley Debates*, pp. 90, 136–7.
[71] *Commons' Journals*, I, p. 811 ; *Fawsley Debates*, p. 137.
[72] *Fawsley Debates*, p. 137 ; see also p. 143, " Yet for all these things
he cannot consent to give at this time, but hereafter."

for a petition to the King, to sit " ; " the proper resolution now is, whether we shall desire to sit now for these things, or to recede. And that ariseth out of his Majesty's gracious offer either to sit now or at winter ; God forbid that we should deny his Majesty supply if there be cause, and he moveth that we should petition to debate these things at winter." [73] But, if " these things " included supply as, indeed, would appear from the context, no grant would be voted at Oxford. Nor does he, I think, express " willingness." " He doth not think that there is such a necessity as is pretended." He does, indeed, say " God forbid that we should deny his Majesty supply if there be cause," " yet God forbid we should be so limited, that, upon whatsoever occasion, we should give no more." [74] But what of the first of these points, if, indeed, there was no need for more? And the second appears to mean only that Eliot went not so far as to say he would *never* give more, whatsoever might be the conditions. Gardiner suppresses his motion. Why suppress so important a matter? I must quote the remarks in his preface : " Eliot's speech, in fact, reduced itself to this : There are grave doubts about the policy of the Government. But do not let us be drawn aside by personal questions or legal technicalities from our plain duty of finding out what is really needed, in order that we may at once supply the need." [75] This passage is wholly beyond me, as is also this statement by Forster, unless he misconstrued the *Journals,* " Eliot rose with a proposition for an address to the King for permission to continue to sit." [76] Strode's meaning is not very clear. Nor, again, are reporters agreed as to which of the two Strodes it was, if, indeed, only one of them spoke. For the *Fawsley Debates* say Sir William, the appendix and *Journals* " Mr. " Strode. I will give the reports in a note, that the reader himself may consider what

[73] *Commons' Journals,* I, p. 811 ; *Fawsley Debates,* p. 138. " Eliot followed," says Gardiner. " It was his last appearance as a mediator " (*History,* V, p. 413).
[74] *Fawsley Debates,* pp. 137–8.
[75] *Ibid.,* p. xvi.
[76] *Sir John Eliot,* I, p. 387.

bearing they have on the issue.[77]   For that matter both may
have spoken.   Nathaniel Rich brought up the rear.   His
advice, so the *Journals* inform us, was " not to refuse to give :
but first to represent to the King our wants."   Then he followed this up with " five heads."   A Committee should deal
with these " heads," upon which they should frame a
petition, and this should be taken to Charles.   What precisely
would happen thereafter is no easy thing to determine.   But,
it seems, they must have the King's answer before they
debated supply : " and that answer being obtained we shall
be the fitter to resolve the question of supply."   The writer
of the *Fawsley Debates* in the margin has " conditional
subsidies."   When was " that answer " expected?   " If it be
objected we shall not have time enough, the course anciently
was to present the heads of their petitions, and to expect
an answer at the next meeting."   This certainly seems to
suggest that no answer was expected at Oxford and, therefore,
no supply would be voted.   But if Rich contemplated a grant,
while the parliament was sitting at Oxford, on obtaining con-
cessions from Charles, he was not in agreement with Eliot.
One further point about Rich.   The *Journals* said " not to
refuse."   But another report is more definite : " Some move
to give, and give presently, and some would not give at all,
and some would give *sub modo* ; and a 4th (to which he
inclineth) is, that we should first move the King for his answer
to our petition [the petition for religion], for we can have no
hope of a blessing so long as the execrable thing remaineth
amongst us, and to have his Majesty's answer in parliament,
and after a parliamentary way."   Thus he plainly declined

---

[77] " Mr. Strode moveth a grand committee presently, to consider of the
King's supply; and that all, that speak, may apply themselves to this,
how the two subsidies, and fifteens, payable more than one year hence,
can supply the Navy, to go out within fourteen days " (*Commons'
Journals*, I, p. 811).   " Sir Wm. Stroude.   How can two subsidies to be
paid a year hence conduce to the going out of the navy within this
fortnight? " (*Fawsley Debates*, p. 90).   " Mr. Stroude.   The matter con-
sisteth of two things, the King's desire to us, and our desire to the King;
the King's first to be preferred " (*Fawsley Debates*, p. 138).   We find in
one report of the 5th " Sir W[illia]m Strode.   No subsidies, but an humble
remonstrance " (*Fawsley Debates*, p. 135).

" to give presently," " presently " meaning " at once." [78]   For
the statements propounded by Gardiner I so far can see little
warrant.   One other point merits attention.   The House did
not break up that day before Phelips, as one report has it,
" commended the platform of Sir Nathaniel Rich." [79]

If Nethersole is any authority, this debate had but little
significance.   " The next day, into which the further debate
of this business had been deferred, there was not much said
concerning the giving of subsidies, but there were some who
had ill fortune in going about to wipe off those aspersions
which they conceived had been cast on my Lord Duke; one
of them let the House know that his Grace did not execute
the office of admiral by himself, but by certain Commissioners
who were to be blamed for any errors [which] might have
been committed in the preparation of this fleet, which he
seemed to grant."   And then he goes on about Clarke.[80]
Thus, it seems, the discussion was short and had no special
meaning for the writer.   The Clarke case he finds more
important.   And yet, if those five men attempted to come to
some agreement with Buckingham, it seems to me very
unlikely he should have had no knowledge of it.   There was,
too, according to Gardiner, "a tacit agreement to allow a body
of mediators to declare the terms."   How could such an
" agreement " be effective, unless it were made known beforehand to men of the standing of Nethersole, who, for that
matter, had spoken in plain terms the previous morning?   Sir
John Coke is still more in point.   If " a tacit agreement " was
reached, not to mention the Duke's being privy, then Coke
must have been in the secret.   Yet, when Eliot exonerates the
Duke, Coke is up in a moment protesting, " This tax of the
commissioners is an artificial condemning of my Lord
Admiral.   The King's navy is the most potent navy of
Christendom, and if there [be] any thanks deserved, it is all
due to my Lo[rd] Admiral."   Moreover, Coke roundly
declared " that there is no fault in the provision thereof, and

---

[78] *Commons' Journals*, I, p. 811 ; *Fawsley Debates*, pp. 90–1, 138–9.
[79] *Fawsley Debates*, p. 140.
[80] Nethersole to Carleton, August 9 ; *Fawsley Debates*, p. 157.

desireth it may be searched into and examined, and his and their credits who have been employed in it, to stand or fall as it should appear unto the house." [81]   Was that part of " the tacit agreement "?   If Weston, Heath, Edmondes were silent —all spoke on the previous morning, and they may have had no more to say—yet we know that, at least, Coke was not. It would seem he was even indignant.

But, granted that all should have spoken, I doubt whether Gardiner's conclusion could be reasonably drawn from their silence. " After this," to quote Gardiner's admission, " came Clerke, with his violent language throwing the debate into confusion.[82]   Whether that is quite fair to the speaker we need not stay here to inquire. It is reasonable, however, to suppose that other matters might soon be lost sight of, before men like Weston could speak.   Then, again, we may ask what was novel in what was now called Rich's " platform."   That " platform," it seems, was as follows : " 1. For religion ; to have his Majesty's answer in full Parliament, and enrolled ; which then of the force of an Act of Parliament.[83]   2. To know the enemy, against whom our war is to be made. 3. The necessity of an advised council, for government of the great affairs of the Kingdom.   4. The necessity of looking into the King's estate.   5. To have his Majesty's answer concerning impositions." [84]   Weston, when replying to Phelips, declared that " concerning religion, he doubted not that the King would quickly satisfy us.   What was meant by the exception against the counsels near the King, he said he understood not." [85]   " A grave and wise counsel," again, was what Seymour himself had demanded, wherein he was merely repeating what Phelips had said at Westminster.[86] " We know not our enemy," said Seymour.[87] " No enemy yet known," said Coke.[88]   Coke also devoted much time to reforming the

[81] *Fawsley Debates,* pp. 90, 138.   " Doun " is presumably " due " in the first of the passages cited.
[82] *Ibid.,* p. xvi.
[83] Note this particular phrase, which might well be applied to addresses.
[84] *Commons' Journals,* I, p. 811.
[85] *Fawsley Debates,* p. 82 ; August the 4th.
[86] *Ibid.,* pp. 78, 31.
[87] See note 85, *supra.*
[88] *Fawsley Debates,* p. 84.

King's estate, while Phelips had made "impositions" a prominent point in his speech.[89] There was nothing, then, new in the "heads." Nor, again, was there anything novel in setting them down upon paper and framing a petition to the King. Did not Phelips conclude on the 5th "with a motion for a select committee to frame a petition to his Majesty upon such heads as may be for his honour"?[90] Hence, I think, his approval next morning of what he then called Rich's "platform." If, indeed, there was anything novel in the speeches delivered on the 6th, I suspect it was Eliot's motion, though, perhaps, not the feeling behind it. And so it seems hardly surprising, if Nethersole saw no importance in the speeches delivered that morning. The tactics employed by the Commons were marked by a measured monotony. Those heads, then, contained nothing new. But this undermines Gardiner's distinction between "the advanced" or left "wing" and the moderate men in the Commons. Rich was out-Heroding Herod. He dared to put into one speech what some others but touched on in turn. I find at least one point in common in Rich's and Eliot's speeches. "Let us receive truly," says Eliot, "that which belongeth to subjects, which he thinketh his Majesty will yield us, and we shall do that that is fit to reduce it to some heads." This immediately precedes what I quoted, "the proper resolution, etc." "And as for that objection," said Rich, "that the time is not now fitting, it will require a longer time than we may sit here, he thinketh not so, for a committee might be named to digest into heads, which might be presented unto his Majesty, and at this time to capitulate with the King, being never had the subject more cause to do it than we have now."[91] Both speakers are for drawing up "heads," or, in other words, both are in favour of presenting a petition to the King. If the two men had really one plan, I suggest that it may have been threefold. The Commons would draw two petitions, one including the five propositions

[89] *Fawsley Debates*, pp. 85–7, 81.
[90] *Ibid.*, p. 82.
[91] *Fawsley Debates*, pp. 138–9.

and one for postponement till winter. Besides, they would make protestation of " willingness " to grant on conditions when they thus met again some months later.[92]

Some remarks Gardiner makes about Mildmay should not, as I think, be passed over. " Mildmay," he says of his speech, " had quietly thrown overboard all the King's Continental alliances." [93] But why should he throw them all over, when money was not required for them? The money was sought for the navy. Again, we read later of Rich that " he rose to put Mildmay's proposal in a more definite form." [94] This, I fear, is entirely beyond me.

Whatever the facts may have been, the main issues remain unaffected. The Commons showed no disposition at any time during the sittings to fulfil their own plain obligations. Their pledges had been unconditional, provided there should be " a real war." Their address had said nothing whatever concerning " conditional subsidies," not to say subsidies conditional on answers about " impositions." And Heath, as we saw, waived that matter, when dealing with tonnage and poundage. If the Commons would know of the enemy, then Buckingham replied on the 8th : " Make the fleet ready to go ; my master gave me command to bid you name the enemy your selves." [95] But as for those other " propositions," could either the King or the Duke acquiesce in that grave breach of faith they so plainly—nay, blatantly—covered? To " make the fleet ready to go " was the one thing the Commons declined.[96] They had brought the Crown into the war on the strength of unconditional pledges. They broke

---

[92] If a compromise was really attempted, I single out Fleetwood, not Mildmay. See his speech upon August the 8th and the way it was welcomed by Pym (*Fawsley Debates*, pp. 140–1). Fleetwood, perhaps I should add, was Receiver of the Court of Wards.

[93] *History*, V, p. 413.

[94] *Ibid.*, V, p. 414.

[95] *Fawsley Debates*, p. 102 ; *Lords' Journals*, III, p. 484.

[96] I have made, as the reader may notice, no reference to Eliot's tract. I confess I suspect all he tells us, save when it is borne out by others. The passage is quoted in full in the preface to the *Fawsley Debates* (p. xviii). But, even if based upon fact, it refers to attempts at a compromise *after* debate on the 6th and, therefore, in no way affects what was said in the House on that date.

them to suit their own ends, and they left the young King in the lurch with grave debts and an empty exchequer.

THE DISSOLUTION

That Parliament would soon be dissolved became known on the night of the 11th.[97] Let me quote the King's account of the matter, put out in the following year : " His Majesty therefore on the eleventh of July then following, adjourned the Parliament from Westminster, until the first day of August then following, at the city of Oxford; and his Highness was so careful to accommodate his Lords and Commons there, that as he made choice of that place, being then the freest of all others from the danger of that grievous sickness, so he there fitted the Parliament men with all things convenient for their entertainment; and his Majesty himself being in his own heart sincere and free from all ends upon his people (which the searcher of hearts best knows), he little expected that any misconstruction of his actions would have been made, as he there found. But when the Parliament had been a while there assembled, and his Majesty's affairs opened unto them, and a further supply desired, as necessity required, he [98] found them so slow, and so full of delays, and diversions in their resolutions, that before anything could be determined, the fearful contagion daily increased, and was dispersed into all the parts of the Kingdom, and came home even to their doors where they were assembled. His Majesty therefore rather preferred the safety of his people from that present and visible danger, than the providing for that which was more remote, but no less dangerous to the state of this Kingdom, and of the affairs of that part of Christendom, which then were, and yet are in friendship and alliance with his Majesty : and thereupon his Majesty not being able to discern when it might please God to stay his hand of visitation, nor what place might be more secure than other at a time convenient for their reassembling, his Majesty dissolved the

---

[97] Nethersole to Carleton, August 14; *Fawsley Debates*, p. 162.
[98] "And" in the *Bibliotheca* is clearly a misprint for "he"; see Rushworth.

Parliament." [99] This account answers both the main questions, for why did the King end the sittings and end them by dissolving the parliament? The Commons so " misconstrued " his actions and thus, as he says, were " so slow and so full of delays and diversions," that the plague even came to their doors. Moreover, he could not " discern when it might please God to stay his hand of visitation, nor what place might be more secure than other at a time convenient for their reassembling." He would neither prorogue nor adjourn them. Simple, indeed, as it seems, I suggest that this account is correct and the " causes " sufficient and final.

Let us for a moment go back to the message from the King on the 10th. Said the *Fawsley Debates,* as we saw : " His desire is that you will presently resolve whether, upon the important reasons delivered unto us, so much importing his honour, you will supply his necessity in such a proportion that he may send his navy; otherwise, if this will not move you, his Majesty will take more care of your safety than your selves, because the sickness disperseth in this town, and he will do all as well as he may in such an extremity, wherein he may so much suffer. But if you will give a present dispatch of the supply, he doth promise, in the word of a King, giving you that royal word which he had never yet broken, nor given cause to mistrust, that you shall meet again in the winter in a more seasonable time, and stay together till you may bring to maturity those things which were propounded; and that his Majesty will then do whatsoever belongs to a good and gracious King." [100] " His Majesty will take more care of your safety than yourselves, because the sickness disperseth in this town "; " his Majesty therefore rather preferred the safety of his people from that present and visible danger "; " the fearful contagion daily increased, and was dispersed into all the parts of the Kingdom, and came home even to their doors where they were assembled." The later account and the message are so far completely consistent. The message, however, referred to a session to be held in the winter, if supply was immediately

[99] *Bibliotheca Regia,* p. 359 ; Rushworth, p. 408.
[100] See p. 94, *supra.*

I

granted. Nay, Phelips thought adjournment intended, although no supply should be voted, or at least he pretended to think so. " The point being now, by this message, reduced short to this ; either to give presently, or else, that in respect of our danger, he will adjourn us to some other time." And Wentworth, too, spoke of " this manner, to put us upon these slights to give, or else to adjourn," thus discerning a threat in the message.[101] But the message said nothing like that. Let us see what it did say more fully. The report in the *Fawsley Debates* omits one point of vital importance. Both the *Journals* and a letter from Nethersole agree that the session in winter should be at what time they should please, if a " present " supply was forthcoming : " If will now give, giveth his royal word, that in winter, at what time we shall choose, we shall meet again, and hold together, till we have perfected all these things for the Commonwealth, and the King, which are now in conception ; and give such answer thereunto, as dutiful and loving subjects may expect from a gracious and religious King " ; " he therefore prayed us to give him a speedy answer, assuring us that if it were such as he hoped for to supply his present occasions, we should have another session in winter at what time soever we ourselves would appoint it, to consider of the reformation of all those things whereof we could make complaint, and that he would give free way thereunto, engaging his royal word to us for this." [102] This fact is omitted by Gardiner.[103] But let us be clear on one point. Here was no unconditional offer to call them together in winter. The promise was plain and explicit but also in two ways conditioned. Let supply be immediately voted ; he would summon them again in the winter ; they must name their own time for the meeting ; they should sit till their business was finished. But why must they choose their own time ? I suspect that the reason was this, that he would not himself again choose it, while conditions remained as they were and the plague as yet stalked through the land.

[101] *Commons' Journals,* I, p. 814 ; *Fawsley Debates,* p. 113.
[102] *Commons' Journals,* I, p. 813 ; Nethersole to Carleton, August 11, *Fawsley Debates,* p. 159.
[103] *History,* V, p. 423.

They complained of the summons to Oxford, when the King chose the place and the time; not again should they have such a grievance. He would also avoid a dilemma. Suppose that he named a new date and the plague was still raging in winter. If he brought them in spite of it together, they were certain again to condemn him as having no care for their safety. If, however, he postponed the summons, they would none the less surely condemn him as having no care for his pledges. The offer of August the 10th is in many respects on a level with that of the 18th of June—" and the next shall be theirs, as long and as soon as they will, for domestic business." [104]

This message, be it carefully noted, was repeated next morning by Weston, though yet again Gardiner says nothing.[105] We read in the *Fawsley Debates*: " The House was turned into a committee. In the Great Committee it was moved that the King's message might be repeated, and that motion opposed by Sir Tho[mas] Wentworth, and others: but after some debate it was admitted." [106] Says a fuller report: " The house resolved themselves to a committee, and debated the same again, whether to give or not to give, Mr. Solicitor being put in the chair. Sir Nathaniel Rich moveth to have the letter or message of the King declared or repeated, again by Mr. Chancellor, which the house much opposed, but in the end consented unto it; and it was done by Mr. Chancellor; and it was added by Mr. Chancellor, that the King did promise, in the word of King, whereof he had been and ever would be very jealous, to perform unto us what he said, viz. that we should meet again in committee, and debate these businesses we had entered into; and that if we did now give, he would take more care of our healths than we did our selves; and desired the house that they would take to heart what to do in it, whether to give or not, or what return to make to the King." [107] Not only was the message repeated. This also was added by Weston, " that if we did

[104] See p. 21, *supra*.
[105] See *History*, V, p. 429.
[106] *Fawsley Debates*, p. 120.
[107] *Ibid.*, p. 143.

now give, he would take more care of our healths than we did our selves." On the previous morning he said, " Otherwise, if this will not move you, his Majesty will take more care." Now, however, if this is correct, " his Majesty would take more care," whether money were voted or not. Thus the King, in effect, had announced his intention of ending the sittings, and the purpose of Weston's " addition," I think, was to bring out that point. It was surely implicit on the 10th. Therefore, Phelips and Wentworth were wrong. Both were wrong in supposing adjournment an alternative to voting the money, and Wentworth was wrong in supposing the message constituted a threat. But how would the sittings be ended, should supply not at once be forthcoming? The message, we saw, contained nothing about prorogation or adjournment, " if this," as it said, " will not move you "; nor can I believe them intended. If Charles did not mean dissolution, should the offer he made be rejected, the House would again come together; his offer would then have no merit and came, in effect, to his saying that, failing a " present " supply, he would choose his own time for their meeting and would, when he pleased, cut it short.

The King's offer, we saw, was still open on the morning of August the 11th. Now we note this additional point: it was *after* the debate on the pirates and the "naming" by Seymour of Buckingham that the Commons went into committee and the offer was repeated by Weston.[108] Not then could a final decision have been taken about dissolution in the nature of fixing the time. This, again, is omitted by Gardiner. But what was the Commons' response to the offer repeated by Weston? So far as, at least, I can judge, there was less disposition than ever to afford the King any assistance. Nay more, there were some of the speakers for voting " a humble remonstrance "—Seymour and Alford and Puckering—and Alford was repeating a motion he made in debate on the 5th.[109] It was not, indeed, on the 11th that that ominous phrase was first uttered. And once more no question was put.

[108] *Fawsley Debates*, pp. 118, 120.
[109] *Ibid.*, pp. 146, 135.

They would make no immediate grant, and, in fact, they would not grant at all and were turning again to "remonstrance." Charles's offer, in consequence, lapsed. No alternative remained to dissolution, which, I think, would thus follow automatically. No Council would really be needed. To prorogue, to adjourn, to continue would have made the King's message ridiculous. Only one thing was now left—that the King should "make out his commission." When members met again on the morrow, we are told, "It was commonly known that the King had made out his commission for dissolving the Parliament." [110]

Should the reader still think that the plague had been used by the King as a pretext, let these further points be well weighed. Charles had said upon August the 4th: "Here then to hold you long, against your own desires, were to express in me little care of your safeties; and to adjourn it without your further helps were to destroy the preparations already made." [111] He spoke at that time of "adjournment," but the statement was made when the Commons had not yet debated supply and what were their views and their feelings, what course the proceedings would take, were but matters at best of conjecture. But the speeches delivered next morning would surely convince him not only that the summons to Oxford was resented but that "here to hold you long" would be far from agreeable to them. It was Whistler who began the discussion, and Whistler was member for Oxford; he began with "the danger of the plague." [112] That this was in all men's minds we may learn from a letter from Nethersole.[113] Bitter language was held of the summons; we saw the remarks made by Seymour.[114] "For the giving of any at all," so Nethersole says in his letter, "was opposed by three or four of the principal speakers who usually stand stiffest for the

[110] *Ibid.*, p. 124.
[111] See p. 86, *supra*. That adjournment was then in his mind Coke's letter to Brooke also proves—"to leave it to their judgment whether they would now proceed to a resolution or adjourn till winter in regard of the sickness" (*Coke MSS.*, I, p. 208).
[112] *Commons' Journals*, I, p. 810; *Fawsley Debates*, p. 77.
[113] To Carleton, August 9, *Fawsley Debates*, pp. 155–6.
[114] See p. 98, *supra*.

country, and in such a manner as they all shewed a great dislike of our being called hither upon this occasion." From the 5th the contagion was spreading. When the Lords sent a message on the 8th that the King had commanded the Duke to speak in his name to both Houses, we read in the *House of Commons' Journals* of " doubt being made about the place, in respect of the danger." [115]   " The sickness disperseth in this town," said the message by Weston on the 10th. " The fearful contagion daily increased, and was dispersed into all the parts of the Kingdom and came home even to their doors where they were assembled." Whatever they exactly referred to, the last words were no flight of rhetoric. One account of the sittings at Oxford concludes with the following sentence : " (Memorandum.) That whiles we were at Oxford, notwithstanding that the plague was dispersed in the town in six or seven places, and that divers died there whiles we were there, yet no parliament man died of it nor any belonging to the house of Commons but only Sir William Beecher's man; whereupon Sir William Beecher absented himself presently from the house, and came not into the house after again." [116] Since such was the state of affairs, no wonder, if Charles had declined to appoint a further sitting of parliament. Concerned as he was, too, for others, he was also concerned for himself, and he well may have feared the disease, though he feared neither violence nor death. He may also have felt it his duty not to place his own life in grave danger, when nothing could be gained by so doing. " And no longer to endanger our lives to no purpose by holding us together in this place " is in Nethersole's report of his message.[117] We have seen his departure from London.[118] And we learn from a contemporary letter that " at Woodstock, where the Court is, none may go from thence to return, nor any come thither,

[115] *Commons' Journals*, I, p. 812.

[116] *Fawsley Debates*, p. 151. And Nethersole wrote on the 9th, " Sir W. Beecher hath had a man dead of it in this town, whereupon he, being a Parliament man, is removed " *(F.D.,* p. 159). This was on or before August 9.

[117] *Ibid.,* p. 159.

[118] See p. 82, *supra.*

and for contraveners a gibbet is set up at the Court gate."
One way of suspending the infection! [119]

The King's account thus holds the field till we show some
grave reason against it. Unhappily brief as it is, it admits of
a reasonable construction, consistent, it seems, with known
facts. The whole paper of which it forms part is described by
the King in these terms: " a true, plain, and clear Declaration of the causes which moved his Majesty to assemble, and
after enforced him to dissolve these Parliaments." [120] The
whole appears businesslike, honest, unaffected, devoid of all
rhetoric. What is said of the second of these parliaments I see
little reason for doubting. Why doubt what is said of the
first? Prima facie, its very simplicity—politicians might well
call it naïveté—seems to me much in its favour. There was
no lack of other grave causes, had Charles, in fact, cared to
act on them, to make a more telling indictment, when he
came to sum up the whole matter.

That parliament would now be dissolved became known on
the night of the 11th. Buckingham was " named " on that
day, and the two facts are sometimes connected as cause and
effect by historians; the King made some sudden decision.[121]
But, if my account is correct, the decision to dissolve had been
taken, were supply not immediately granted, before Weston's
message on the 10th and could not have been prompted in
that case by what happened later in parliament. At most the

[119] Locke to Carleton, August 14; *State Papers Domestic,* 1625, 1626,
p. 84.
[120] *Bibliotheca Regia,* p. 356; Rushworth, p. 406.
[121] See, for instance, the following statements, which seemingly bear
this construction: 'At length Seymour said the fateful word, 'Let us
lay the fault where it is'; the Duke of Buckingham or his agents were
to blame. The safety of the Kingdom, urged Phelips, was not to be
entrusted to incompetent persons. After this, an agreement was impossible; and on August 12, 1625, Parliament was dissolved" *(Cambridge
Modern History,* IV, p. 261); "The first Parliament skirmished and
bickered, mainly on religion and on the failure of the foreign policy; at
last it went straight to the point and named the Duke of Buckingham.
The King, against his favourite's advice, at once dissolved it" (C. R. L.
Fletcher, *An Introductory History of England from Henry VII to the
Restoration,* p. 290). "The first Parliament skirmished and bickered"
seems, indeed, a most curious summary of all its revolutionary proceedings, and Buckingham was " named " in connection, as a matter of fact,
with the pirates. See *Fawsley Debates,* pp. 117-18.

events of the 11th could but hasten the end by a little. And *after* the naming of Buckingham Weston repeated his message and also, it seems, amplified it.[122] Moreover, we have seen that it was likely that the Duke had been " named " before that. Be it added that the opposite theory must either ignore Weston's message or take up the view that that message contemplated prorogation or adjournment, even though a supply was not voted. I conclude that for these and other reasons this view can have little foundation.

" THE BREAKING OF PARLIAMENT "

I propose at this point to add a chapter, to which we may fitly consign certain views of " the breaking of parliament." Forster again follows Eliot. What, then, is Forster's account? [123] It amounts, I think, briefly to this. Both Phelips and Eliot on the 10th were for making a remonstrance to the King, and the motion was supported by Glanville. In spite of opposition from Weston, a remonstrance in the end was resolved on. A council was called shortly after, and Williams was against dissolution. The Duke, though professing indifference, had rather the sittings continued, since the object of continuing the sittings was to make an attempt on himself. The Lord Keeper protested again. Then the Duke threw himself on his knees and implored the King not to dissolve but, in doing so, acted a part, deprecating what most he desired. Charles was, however, immovable. Though yielding so far to the Duke as to grant a brief respite to the Commons, the drafting and presenting the remonstrance must at all costs, he said, be prevented. Heath should make answer to Mansell and Coke again ask for supply, and convey another message from Charles. A commission was in secret prepared and, when Sherland had spoken next morning,[124] was immediately handed to Williams with instructions at once to discharge it.

---

[122] *Fawsley Debates*, pp. 118, 120.
[123] *Sir John Eliot*, I, pp. 407-40.
[124] Forster for Sherland says Littleton, following Eliot's statements. See *Sir John Eliot*, I, p. 433 : "Littleton was called up by a speech from Sir Humphrey May." We may add that May spoke on the 10th, not, as this would suggest, on the 12th.

Some delay was, however, occasioned by a conference between the two Houses, and the Commons could not be prevented from sitting again on the 12th. When the news of what now was in store reached their ears on the same afternoon, " some distraction was wrought in their mind." [125]

This story seems palpably false. It is full of the grossest misstatements. That Eliot seconded Phelips has now, once for all, been disproved. He did not speak at all on the 10th. He inserted a speech never spoken in the record he gives of that sitting. This fact is admitted by Gardiner, the first, for that matter, to note it.[126] And Phelips proposed no remonstrance. He " concluded," we read, " with two motions. 1. That Sir Ro[bert] Mansell might be commanded to declare his knowledge with what deliberation and counsel this design [of the fleet] hath been managed. 2. To appoint a committee to prepare an answer for his Majesty, and reasons why we cannot give." [127] As for Glanville, we are told he concluded " for the drawing a petition which might be accompanied with some such protestation as shall credit the King more than 60,000 pounds." [128] Nor did they " conclude for a remonstrance." [129] " This long debate ended only in this order, That the House to-morrow morning should sit in a committee to consider what return to make to the King." [130] That is certainly positive enough and is borne out by Seymour and Heath. For the former observed the next morning, " It was not the meaning of the house (as he conceiveth) that this

[125] *Sir John Eliot*, I, p. 440.
[126] *Fawsley Debates*, p. xx; *History*, V, p. 425, note 1.
[127] *Fawsley Debates*, p. 110; see the *Journals*, I, p. 814: " Moveth, Sir Ro. Mansell may deliver his opinion of the designs in hand ; and a Committee, to consider of a fit answer to his Majesty, why we cannot now give ; and yet to give him assurance, we will, in due time, supply all his honourable and well-grounded designs."
[128] *Fawsley Debates*, p. 115; see the *Journals*, I, p. 814: " Moveth, a Committee to consider a satisfactory answer to his Majesty ; with some protestation (without engagement) that we will, in due time, supply."
[129] See *Negotium Posterorum*, I, p. 93.
[130] *Fawsley Debates*, p. 116; see the *Journals*, I, p. 814: " Resolved, a Committee of the whole House, at eight of the clock to-morrow morning, to consider what return to make to his Majesty's message delivered this day." Forster says the *Journals* are wrong, as they would be, were Eliot right. But the *Fawsley Debates* bears them out, as (see later) does Nethersole also. See *Sir John Eliot*, I, p. 427, footnote.

committee should debate whether to give or not to give, and to enter into a new debate of it, and the reasons thereof, either for necessity or profit; but the order was, that the house should enter into consideration for the manner of their answer, and therefore read the order," while later we find Heath remarking, " We are now in a debate what answer to make unto the King." [131] Nethersole describes the debate that took place in the House on the 10th. Not a word does he say of a remonstrance. He writes of the end of the sitting : " Thereupon the question having been declined again, the debate was put off till this day." [132] So much for what passed in debate. They were always " declining the question." What, then, of the rest of the tale? No remonstrance was mentioned that day. Why should Charles, then, insist the same day on preventing remonstrance at all costs? We saw that on *August the 5th* Alford moved for " a humble remonstrance " and, it seems, was supported by Strode.[133] Then it was for the King to take steps, not to suffer five days to pass over, if he really desired to forestall it. Heath answered Mansell on the 12th, though we should, if this account is correct, have been naturally led to expect he would do so upon the 11th.[134] Coke did not ask for supply nor, it seems, speak again in the House. His alleged speech appears to be Marten's.[135] The Commons are said to have learnt on the *afternoon* of August the 11th that the King had made out his commission. But Nethersole says, "the same night."[136] For the conference with the Lords about religion, it was actually held on the 10th and could hardly, so far as I can see, have delayed the impending dissolution.[137] The whole story, indeed, seems discredited. We cannot but ask, too, how Eliot discovered what passed in the Council. Did someone betray

[131] *Fawsley Debates*, pp. 145, 146.

[132] To Carleton, August 11 ; *Fawsley Debates*, p. 61.

[133] See p. 116, *supra*.

[134] *Fawsley Debates*, p. 122 ; Nethersole to Carleton, August 14, *F.D.*, p. 162.

[135] *Sir John Eliot*, I, p. 430 ; *Fawsley Debates*, pp. 120, 143, xxiv.

[136] See p. 112, *supra:* " The same night we had certain knowledge that the Parliament would be dissolved the next morning, and that affected men's minds as you imagine."

[137] *Lords' Journals*, III, p. 487.

the King's business? Who told the opponents of Buckingham that he went on his knees to the King? Who knew of the Duke's secret longings, that not even Charles seemed aware of?

So far as this curious story relates to the King's Privy Council, I find it adopted by Gardiner, who tacitly alters the date. For he places it on the 11th. "That afternoon," he writes in his *History,* "the Council met to consider whether the House should be allowed to sit any longer. Once more Williams pleaded hard against the fatal error of opening a new reign with a quarrel with the House of Commons. For once Buckingham was on the same side. Throwing himself on his knees he entreated the King to allow the Parliament to continue; but Charles was immovable, and the dissolution was irrevocably determined on." In the main, that is Eliot's story. Indeed, he continues as follows, appealing to Eliot's *Negotium:* "Buckingham's petition was naturally described by his opponents as a mere piece of acting," a view he gives reason for doubting.[138] But assuredly Gardiner's procedure, to say least, is wholly uncritical. We saw that he alters the date, just as though that were quite immaterial, and does so without any warning. But he thereby upsets the whole tale. What becomes of the further brief respite conceded by the King to the Duke? That respite was possible only, if the Council was held on the 10th. If, again, it was held the next day, it were meaningless to say, as says Forster, that "another day's sitting of the commons could not be prevented."[139] But Gardiner ignores all these points. And the same fate befalls the remonstrance and all the false statements we noted in regard to debate on the 10th. By what critical canons does Gardiner, while rejecting the date and much else, yet accept the main points in this story?

Did Buckingham oppose dissolution? On the part that he played at that time none can reconcile Hacket with Eliot. This brings me to Hacket's short notice. "*The Commons of this Parliament was censur'd at* Woodstock *for spiteful, and*

---

[138] *History,* V, pp. 429-30.
[139] *Sir John Eliot,* I, p. 439.

seditious: therefore not fit to continue, but to be dissolv'd. Which Resolution being brought to the Clerk of the Crown, to dissolve them on the 12th of August; the Keeper did never so bestir him since he was born, as to turn the Tide, with Reasons, with Supplications, with Tears, imploring his Majesty to remember a time, when, in his hearing, his blessed Father had charg'd him to call Parliaments often, and continue them, though their rashness sometimes did offend him; that in his own Experience, he never got good by falling out with them. *But chiefly Sir,* says he, *let it never be said,* that you have not kept good Correspondence with your first *Parliament. Do not disseminate so much unkindness through all the Counties, and Boroughs of your Realm. The Love of the People is the Palladium of your Crown. Continue this Assembly to another Session, and expect alteration for the better. If you do not so, the next swarm will come out of the same Hive.* To this the Lords of the Council did almost all concur; but it wanted *Buckingham's* Suffrage: who was secure that the King's Judgment would follow him against all the Table. So this first Parliament was blasted, *Et radicis vitium in fructibus nascentibus ostenditur."* [140]

So short and so vague are these statements that I find them not easy to follow. " The Commons of this Parliament was censured at Woodstock "—" censured," I suppose, by the King or, if not, by the Duke or by both. " Therefore not fit to continue, but to be dissolved. Which resolution being brought to the Clerk of the Crown, to dissolve them on the 12th of August, the Keeper did never so bestir him, etc." The decision to dissolve on the 12th was, it thus seems, unknown to the Keeper until it was brought to the Clerk. But, if so, then it must have been taken without any meeting at Woodstock or Williams himself had been absent and was ignorant of what had occurred. Then " the Keeper did never so bestir him since he was born, as to turn the tide "—or reverse the decision. What followed? Did Charles call a meeting? But if such a meeting took place, why does Hacket not say so quite

[140] *Scrinia Reserata,* II, p. 16. I quote this exactly as it stands, punctuation, italics and so forth remaining as in Hacket's text.

plainly? How different his account of a meeting at Hampton
on July the 10th![141] What, in short, does he claim to
describe? "The Keeper did never so bestir himself since he
was born." This suggests some elaborate canvass, some
abnormal display of activity. The phrase, indeed, seems far
too strong for a speech and a vote at a meeting. Besides, we
know Hacket's own use. For example, but two pages later,
Williams " bestirr'd him in the former King's Reign, to check
the encroaching of the Commons, about impeaching the great
Peers, and Officers of the Realm, which the Duke fomented in
the Earl of *Middlesex's* Case." " It wanted Buckingham's
suffrage "—so colourless a phrase would be strange in a writer
so brisk and vivacious, if Hacket is describing a meeting.
Could Buckingham, we ask, have been silent? It seems quite
unlike what we know of him. The words might be used to
convey that he ignored the Lord Keeper's activities. " Secure "
—does " secure " here mean " confident "?—" that the
King's judgement would follow him against all the table."
This phrase might apply to a meeting or stand for " against all
the others." " That the King's judgement would follow
him" certainly seems to imply that the King had not made up
his mind or had not been approached in the matter and the
Duke, not the King, had decided to dissolve upon August the
12th. " With reasons, with supplications, with tears, imploring
his Majesty, etc." Did all this take place at a meeting? I
own that for my part I doubt it. We saw the Lord Duke on
his knees; now we see the Lord Keeper in tears. Was the
King's Privy Council hysterical? Were there, if not, two play-
actors? I am, therefore, inclined to conclude that no meeting
is meant in this passage and that Hacket, if he writes from
real knowledge, describes some informal proceedings or is of
set purpose ambiguous. The Keeper's remarks to the King
must themselves make the reader suspicious. " His blessed
father had charged him to call Parliaments often, and continue them, though their rashness sometimes did offend him;
that in his own experience, he never got good by falling out
with them." Prima facie, this seems most unlikely. And

[141] *Ibid.*, II, p. 13.

have we, in Clarendon's *History,* not seen James admonishing Charles and protesting "that he would live to have his bellyful of parliaments"?[142]   If driven to choose as between them, I much prefer Clarendon's story.   And who, for that matter, would not?

Hacket seems vague about dates.   The commission was brought to the Clerk to dissolve them on August the 12th. But when was it brought to the Clerk?   The King's message was repeated on the Thursday; his offer was, therefore, still open.   At that time we, therefore, suppose he had not yet "made out his commission," unless we imagine it already for some reason made out in secret, a view that, for my part at least, I can see no solid ground for assuming.   But granted the commission was brought to the Clerk of the Crown on the Thursday, little time, as it seems, could be left for the Keeper's so strenuous efforts.   For one thing at least appears certain.   That parliament would now be dissolved became known, as we saw, that same night and was known in the city itself.[143]   It was "commonly known" in the House fairly soon on the following morning.[144]

Earlier in August the Keeper, if Hacket's account could be trusted, had gone uninvited to Buckingham.   He told him, among other things, "You have brought the Two Houses hither, my Lord, against my Counsel.   My Suspicion is confirm'd, that your Grace would suffer for it.   What's now to be done? but wind up a Session quickly.   The occasion is for you; because two Colledges in the University, and eight Houses in the City are visited with the Plague.   Let the Members be promis'd fairly and friendly, that they shall meet again after Christmas.   Requite their Injuries done unto you with benefits, and not revenge.   For no Man, that is wise, will shew himself angry with the People of England.   I have more to say, but no more than I have said to your Grace above a Year past at White-hall.   Confer one or two of your great Places upon your fastest Friends : so shall you go less in Envy,

---

[142] See p. 5, *supra.*

[143] Nethersole was writing *from Oxford; Fawsley Debates,* pp. 162, 163.   He wrote three days later from Woodstock.

[144] *Fawsley Debates,* p. 124.

and not less in Power. . . . At the Close of this Session declare your self to be the forwardst to serve the King and Common-wealth, and to give the Parliament satisfaction. Fear them not, when they meet again in the same Body: whose ill Affections I expect to mitigate : but if they proceed, trust me with your Cause, when it is transmitted to the House of Lords, and I will lay my Life upon it, to preserve you from Sentence, or the least Dishonour.   This is my Advice my Lord. If you like it not, Truth in the end will find an Advocate to defend it."   But Buckingham, says Hacket, " replied no more but, *I will look whom I trust to,* and flung out of the Chamber with Minaces in his Countenance." [145]   That the Duke brought the Houses to Oxford is the theory repeated by Hacket in his story about the adjournment and refuted at length in a paper drawn up under Lord Conway's eyes.[146] To find Williams repeating it to Buckingham seems not a little surprising.   " I have more to say, but no more than I have said to your Grace above a year past at Whitehall." This reminds us of his letter to Buckingham, advising him to give up the Admiralty and take up the office of Steward. This letter to Buckingham was dated March 2, 1625; but Hacket thought this was mistaken.   " He that Reads it all, as it is in *Cab.* p. 101. Shall find it no loss of time; mending the Fault of the Date (a mistake very common in that Rhapsody of Letters) it should bear the Style of *Feb.* 13. 1623. instead of *Mart.* 2. 1624." [147]   February, 1624, would, of course, be " above a year past "; but the other date suits the phrase better.   If this is not the source of the statement attributed to Williams by Hacket and Williams, in fact, made the statement and made it at Oxford to Buckingham, he showed a surprising persistence in offering advice so unpalatable.   When, too, did Williams tell Buckingham, " Fear them not, when they meet again in the same body, whose ill affections I expect to mitigate," which reminds us of what Hacket tells us he said upon July the 10th about

---

[145] *Scrinia Reserata,* II, p. 16, nearly all in italics.

[146] This paper is cited in full at the end of the *Fawsley Debates,* pp. 164ff.

[147] *Scrinia Reserata,* I, p. 174 ; " *Cab.*" is presumably *Cabala.*

"undertaking with the sticklers"?[148] If this interview ever took place, I suppose it could hardly be earlier than August the 5th or the 6th, for the Keeper's "suspicion is confirmed, that your Grace would suffer for it." What, however, said Williams of himself in the paper he gave to the King, when the sittings at Oxford were over? " I did the like to my Lord-Duke at *Oxford*, desiring his Lordship to send me his Commands by any trusty Servant, and I would serve him to the utmost of my Power from time to time. His Grace said he would send, but never sent to me. So that if I had any Power in either House (I had much the less at this time by reason of the Paucity of the Lawyers, who were in the Circuit) what use could I make of it without Directions? And to tell the plain truth, I durst do nothing for fear of offending the Duke, otherwise than by Direction. Only 'tis known, that they that were for giving of Subsidies, repaired to me as often as to any other Lord, who can witness of my Care, both in Matters of Subsidies, and the Business of my Lord-Duke. Rationally it was unsafe for me to stickle at this time without Countenance and Employment by, and from your excellent Majesty. . . . I told the Lord-Duke in my Garden, that having been much reprehended by your Majesty, and his Grace in the Earl of *Middlesex's* Tryal, for thanking the last King at *Greenwich,* for promising to protect his Servants, and great Officers against the People and Parliament, I durst not be so active, and stirring by my Friends in that House, as otherwise I should be, unless your Majesty, by his Grace's means, would be pleas'd to encourage me with your Royal Promise, to defend and protect me in your Service. If I might hear your Majesty say so much, I would venture then my Credit, and my Life, to manage what should be entrusted to me to the uttermost. After which he never brought me to your Majesty, nor any Message from you. Standing therefore upon these doubtful terms, unemploy'd in the Duties of my Place (which were now assign'd over to my Lord *Conway,* and Sir *J. Cooke*) and left out of all Committees among the Lords of the Council

[148] *Scrinia Reserata,* II, p. 14.

(which I know was never done by the direction of your Majesty, who ever conceiv'd of me far above my Merit) and consequently fallen much in the Power, and Reputation due to my place, I durst not at this time, with any safety, busie my self in the House of Commons, with any other than that measure of Zeal, which was exprest by the rest of the Lords of the Privy-Council." [149]   If all these protestations are honest, he could hardly, I think, have " expected to mitigate " the Commons' " affections," and, if Hacket's account is correct, then he must have been lying to the Duke.   Then again, his " bestirring himself " as at no time before in his life would appear to be hardly consistent with the attitude disclosed in this paper.   Not only, indeed, in this paper but also in the course of two letters he addressed somewhat later to the King did the Keeper defend his own conduct and in some points apologize for it. [150]   No reference, however, is made to his having opposed dissolution, though he says of " the Meeting at Oxford," " *I oppos'd it at* Hampton-Court, *and* Ricott, *and would have had it put off at* Woodstock." [151]   On the whole, it appears to me safer to place no reliance on Hacket, whose account is, moreover, as striking for much that is simply omitted.   Not a word of the Chancellor's message ; not a word of its being repeated.   It must have been known to the Keeper.   If he really knew what was intended and later opposed dissolution, he was doing the King a disservice and acting, no doubt, in a spirit he was soon at such pains to disclaim.   But I think myself bound to add here that the feeling that is borne in upon me from studying Williams's conduct is that arguments derived from his language are apt to be somewhat precarious.   I suspect he was facile and false, and for once I incline to agree with Mr. Fletcher's outspoken opinion.   He describes him in so many words as " a versatile, unsteady humbug." [152]   If Clarendon's portrait does him justice, he united to other grave vices, unbecoming most of all

---

[149] *Scrinia Reserata,* II, p. 17.
[150] *Ibid.,* II, pp. 20, 24.
[151] *Ibid.,* II, p. 24.
[152] *Introductory History of England from Henry VII to the Restoration.* p. 269.

in a prelate, that of being an inveterate romancer. " He had a faculty of making relations of things done in his own presence, and discourses made to himself, or in his own hearing, with all the circumstances of answers and replies, and upon arguments of great moment; all which, upon examination, were still found to have nothing in them that was real, but to be the pure effect of his own invention." [153] It appears that, according to Coke, his dismissal was generally welcomed. " Your Lordship hath full information of all proceedings concerning the change of the Keeper. He vaunted he could have intercession made for him not only by the most powerful mediators but by the generality of the land. Yet it pleased the good Bishop rather to submit himself to his Majesty's pleasure than to use his strength. By the change his Majesty hath gained a solid and grave counsellor and the Lord Duke hath given the world a very good satisfaction as well by the removing of the one as by the advancement of the other." [154]

To return for a moment to Gardiner. We saw that he writes in his *History*: " That afternoon the Council met to consider whether the House should be allowed to sit any longer," and after the word " afternoon " we observe that he places a 3. Note 3 at the foot is as follows: " Bishop of Mende to Richelieu, received Aug. $\frac{19}{29}$, *King's MSS.* 137, 99. Nethersole to Carleton, Aug. 14, *Fawsley Debates,* 162." [155] This note appears very misleading, for the reader might naturally imagine that Gardiner's account of the Council was derived from the writers referred to. Yet Nethersole's letter has nothing but the sentence I previously quoted—not so much as the mention of a meeting. And as for the Bishop of Mende, this is all that he says of the matter: " Bouquingan [Buckingham] donc se voiant trompé en son dessein et que pour avoir sacriffiés les Catholiques il n'estoit point a Couvert, il fit assembler le Conseil a Ortford [Oxford] le jeudy suivant ou resolution fut prise de rompre le dit Parlement sans avoir Esgard a la necessité de leurs affaires Le Vendredy au matin;

---

[153] *History,* I, p. 489. The whole " character " merits attention.
[154] To Brooke (draft), November 5, 1625; *Coke MSS.,* I, p. 223.
[155] *History,* V, p. 429.

et le Roy apres leur avoir declaré par son Garde des Seaux que Bouquingan n'avoit rien fait que par Son expres Commandem[t] il leur fit enjoindre de se retirer en leurs Maisons." [156]   Gardiner takes the date from the Bishop, rejecting the rest of his statement, which seems to imply very clearly that the Duke was for breaking the parliament. Eliot and the Bishop, in short, are employed to correct one another in a way that seems perfectly arbitrary.

The Bishop, in truth, tells us little. The Duke felt his plan was a failure, for, though he threw over the Catholics, his position was still insecure. So he brought the Privy Council together at Oxford on Thursday, the 11th. Then it was that decision was taken to dissolve upon Friday, the 12th. There are reasons for doubting these statements, apart from the plain implication that Buckingham, fearing opposition, was bent upon saving himself. Though Daniel du Plessis, the Bishop of Mende, was Chief Almoner then to the Queen, we are not justified in assuming without some more positive ground that he knew the Duke's feelings and motives. And what shall we say of the meeting? This point is, at least, worth remarking. No meeting on August the 11th is recorded in the Privy Council Register. A meeting " att Christ's Church in Oxon " is recorded on August the 10th. The Lord Keeper was one of those present, but Charles and the Duke were not there. In so far as the records inform us, the business concerned one John Franklyn.[157] On the whole, then, the good Bishop's letter does not, as I think, help us much.

" The abrupt and ungracious breaking of the two first parliaments," says Clarendon, " was wholly imputed to the duke of Buckingham; and of the third, principally to the lord Weston, then lord high treasurer of England; both in respect of the great power and interest they then had in the affections of his majesty, and for that the time of the dissolu-

---

[156] *King's MSS.*, 137, folio 46. I may add that the references in Gardiner at this stage are not all correct and are also a little misleading. The letter to which he refers in a footnote on p. 415 is, in fact, not the same with the letter referred to on p. 418 and, again, on p. 429. For further details, see Appendix, p. 176.

[157] *P.C.* 2, no. 33, folio 90.

tions happened to be, when some charges and accusations were preparing, and ready to be preferred against those two great persons." [158]   I have had some occasion to remark, in regard to events of this period, that Clarendon is hardly reliable. The case may, however, be different, when he deals with the views or suspicions, that prevailed among men then or later. We note that the breaking of the parliament " was wholly imputed to the Duke." It is not itself stated as fact; it is simply an inference from facts, and no knowledge whatever is pretended of what passed at Court or in Council. If Forster's quotation is reliable, Eliot in his manuscript notes gives a similar account of the matter, instead of the wonderful story set forth, as we saw, in the *Negotium*: " All men possest their neighbours that that meeting was the duke's. That he, to color the follie of his enterprises, had practis'd to entitle them to the parliament. That upon the parliament discovering his practice and corruption, to secure himself therein he had rais'd a jelousie in the King, by w[ch] that breach was made. This was believ'd of all." [159]   But the common belief may be false.

Before we conclude this survey, let me go on in fairness to add what, I think, *might* be plausibly said in reply to the King's declaration. Weston observed on the 5th in the course of debate on supply that " If now we will forsake it, if we do not see this day the effect of our counsel, beyond this day we cannot counsel." [160]   He was " trying," according to Gardiner, " to frighten them with a prospect of dissolution." [161]   The words might be read as a threat, and in that case, of course, we could argue that Weston spoke the mind of the King and the plague was thus merely a pretext. That Weston spoke the mind of the King is at best an unsupported conjecture and seems inconsistent with the fact that adjournment and not dissolution, should the Commons not grant him assistance, was in the King's mind on the 4th. And the natural supposition

[158] *History*, I, p. 7.
[159] *Sir John Eliot*, I, p. 444, note.
[160] *Fawsley Debates*, p. 83.
[161] *History*, V, p. 411.

is that Weston was speaking for none but himself. That his words constituted a threat also seems, to my mind, very doubtful. Debate had but then just begun; it would seem far too soon for a threat. They could not have been literally meant. Though he said and repeated " this day," yet " this day," in fact, brought nothing forth. I suspect he was stating a principle—or, if you prefer it, a maxim. Should those whose advice you accepted deny or go back on their pledges, repudiate solemn engagements, cast public undertakings to the winds, then you cannot sit down again with them and at once ask their counsel afresh.

CHAPTER V

ON the principal questions at issue the history of tonnage and poundage in the next and in subsequent years throws, I think, much additional light. For this point of the customs is vital. None other has so much importance for those who would grasp the real aims of the more "active part" of the Commons, their spirit, their methods, the manner in which they approached their young sovereign. Consider their doings next year, and remember this bill was "their darling." The following occurs in the *Journals* for Tuesday, the 14th of March : "The Bill of Tonnage and Poundage to be brought in by Tuesday next by the King's Counsel; or else the farmers to be sent for, to give account, by what authority they receive it." [1] This direction was, doubtless, complied with. We find on the 24th March that a bill for the grant of the customs was read a second time in the Commons and "committed to a Committee of the whole House; with power to make sub-committees, and with power to send for any customers, books of rates, etc." [2] There was certainly one sub-committee, to which the book of rates was remitted, as we learn from some subsequent entries.[3] Then, we read upon April the 5th, they resolved to proceed with the bill, which was "specially recommended"—whatever we take that to mean—"to be handled the three first days." [4] Of this "handling" I find nothing more. When we come to the 27th April, the bill was again in debate. A remonstrance was suggested by Spencer "concerning the taking of tonnage and poundage without grant in Parliament." This move was, it

---

[1] I, p. 836.
[2] *Commons' Journals*, I, p. 840 ; but nothing about a debate. The first reading seems not to be entered.
[3] *Ibid.*, I, pp. 850, 862.
[4] *Ibid.*, I, p. 844 ; in the margin, "Bills to be proceeded with."

seems, premature. They reserved it "for further debate" and pretended, at least, in the meantime once more "to proceed with" the bill.[5] But again I can find no "proceeding." I find, indeed, no further entry for nearly as much as a month. On the 24th May they discussed what they called a "Petition of Grievance." In this they resolved to include not the pretermitted customs alone but the levying of tonnage and poundage without parliamentary authority; in effect, they pronounced it illegal.[6] On June the 8th, finally, the House, thus reverting to Spencer's proposal, decided on making a remonstrance. To draft it they named a committee, whose work the dissolution of parliament speedily brought to an end.[7]

What, then, we may naturally ask, can be learnt from these few scanty notes? That no bill was intended to pass? First of all, the King's Counsel in the Commons were instructed to bring in a bill and were given a week for the purpose; the farmers, if not, would be sent for; the levies would be certainly questioned and probably made an occasion for a further attack on the Crown. When the bill was brought in, the threat failed. What, then, were the Commons to do? It would seem that they fell back again on the need for a new book of rates, on the pretermitted customs and so on. These questions might cause some delay or at least could be used to occasion it. But can we suppose them in earnest? For twice they resolved to proceed. But did they proceed *with the bill?* They proceeded instead to a remonstrance. Moreover, they shifted their ground. First of all, they would challenge the levies, *unless* their instruction was obeyed and a bill was brought in in a week. Now, however, they would challenge the levies, *although* their instruction was complied with. We found them in the previous summer resolved against granting for life; now we find them to every appearance resolved against granting at all.

Let us here say a word or two more on the Commons'

[5] *Ibid.,* I, p. 850.
[6] *Ibid.,* I, p. 863.
[7] *Ibid.,* I, p. 867; see also pp. 869, 871.

" intended remonstrance." We find it described in the *Journals* for the year 1626 as " a Declaration to the King "— a " Remonstrance," so Rushworth describes it, " or Declaration against the Duke, and concerning Tonnage and Poundage taken by the King since the death of his Father, without consent in Parliament." We come on the following passage, according to the copy in Rushworth : " This intimation, may it please your Majesty, was such as also gave us just cause to fear there were some ill ministers near your Majesty, that in behalf of the said Duke, and together with him, who is so strangely powerful, were so much against the parliamentary course of this kingdom, as they might perhaps advise your most excellent Majesty such new counsels as these, that fell under the memory and consideration of that Privy Counsellor. And one especial reason among others hath increased that fear amongst us. For that whereas the subsidies of tonnage and poundage, which determined upon the death of your most royal father our late sovereign, and were never payable to any of your Majesty's ancestors but only by a special act of Parliament, and ought not to be levied without such an act, yet ever since the beginning of your Majesty's happy reign over us, the said subsidies have been levied by some of your Majesty's ministers, as if they were still due; although also one Parliament hath been since then begun, and dissolved by procurement of the said Duke, as is before shewed, wherein no act passed for the same subsidies. Which example is so much against the constant use of former times, and the known right and liberty of your subjects, that it is an apparent effect of some new counsels given against the ancient settled course of government of this your Majesty's kingdom, and chiefly against the right of your Commons, as if there might be any subsidy, tax or aid levied upon them, without their consent in Parliament, or contrary to the settled laws of this kingdom." [8]

Thus Buckingham was charged more especially with the levying of tonnage and poundage. No act, indeed, passed for that grant. But to whom was that due but to parliament? Charles was in no way to blame. Were the dues to remain

[8] Rushworth, p. 404 ; see also pp. 398 and 400.

uncollected for months—it might well be, for years? In their paper the Commons appealed to " the constant use of former times." But who from that use first departed? They also referred to " new counsels given against the ancient settled course of government of this your Majesty's kingdom." Who but the Commons themselves first resorted to certain " new counsels " in dealing with tonnage and poundage? The collecting of tonnage and poundage without the authority of parliament was not, as a fact, a " new counsel "; this point is brought out very clearly in the King's own account of the matter. And no more ingenuous, surely, is the tacit suggestion that Buckingham, by bringing about a dissolution, prevented an act for those subsidies.

We draw the same moral, I think, from the bill introduced two years later. The Commons were once more engaged in the same disingenuous game. For we find on the 21st March an instruction to bring in a bill.[9] Then the bill, it would seem, was brought in, read a first time on April the 2nd, a second on April the 4th and committed to the House as a whole.[10] On the 9th of the month Bankes reported " from the grand Committee, the Bill concerning Tonnage and Poundage.— That they have all resolved, that there should be a remonstrance made to his Majesty, of our right; and to have a book of rates agreed upon in Parliament; and that . . . A draught read, of a remonstrance to his Majesty, tendered to the said Committee. *Resolved,* To defer, till to-morrow, the resolution of the Committee, and the draught of the said remonstrance. The Bill of Subsidy of Tonnage and Poundage, recommitted to the said Committee." [11] No entry appears on the 10th. On the next day, however, " Mr. Bankes moveth concerning the remonstrance about the settling of impositions. The further consideration of the remonstrance tendered to the House, and of a book of rates, and of all things incident thereunto, referred to the grand Committee for Trade." [12] Then some new books of rates

[9] *Commons' Journals,* I, p. 874.
[10] *Ibid.,* I, pp. 878, 879.
[11] *Ibid.,* I, p. 881.
[12] *Ibid.,* I, p. 882.

" lately printed " were mentioned on May the 17th; Edmond
Sawyer was named a projector and ordered to " bring those
books to the House, if he have any: and the officers of the
custom-house then also to attend with the new books of rates,
if they have any." [13] The *Journals* refer two days later to
" the select Committee for examination of the new books of
rates," which was ordered to meet on the morrow. We find,
too, the same day this entry: " The grand Committee
appointed this day for Tonnage and Poundage, etc., to sit
to-morrow morning." [14] A report from the Committee for
Trade can be found on the 4th day of June and some entries
about impositions on the 7th, 9th, 11th and 13th.[15] On the
9th we read under " Committees " " Tonnage and Poundage :—To-morrow, two clock in the whole House." [16] On the
18th the House in Committee were ordered to deal with the bill
and to deal with it on the next day.[17] On the 19th " the
grand Committee for Tonnage and Poundage " was to sit
in the afternoon.[18] On the 20th " the Committee for
Tonnage and Poundage " was " to sit again to-morrow
morning, nine clock; and the officers of the custom house,
and merchants, then to attend." [19] So again, on the 21st
June, " The Committee for Tonnage and Poundage to sit
presently; and to take consideration of his Majesty's . . .
by Mr. Solicitor, and what fit to be done concerning Sir
Edm. Sawyer, and Sir S. Harvey." Bankes also brought up
a report from the Committee for Tonnage and Poundage
" concerning Sir Edm. Sawyer, about making a new book of
rates "; and Sawyer himself was expelled and, moreover,
was sent to the Tower and declared " unworthy ever to serve
as a member of this House." [20] But the bill had, meanwhile,
been forgotten, and so on the 23rd June they decided to have

---

[13] *Commons' Journals,* I, p. 899.
[14] *Ibid.,* I, p. 900.
[15] *Ibid.,* I, 909, 910, 911, 912.
[16] *Ibid.,* I, p. 910.
[17] *Ibid.,* I, 915.
[18] *Ibid.,* I, p. 915.
[19] *Ibid.,* I, p. 916.
[20] *Commons' Journals,* I, pp. 916, 917. The reader will notice, in
passing, how badly these records were kept.

it "looked up, and a copy gotten, and presented to the Lords
[sic] to-morrow morning"; in addition, "a Grand Committee to-morrow morning, eight clock, to consider of a
course for Tonnage and Poundage, etc." [21]   And two days
later we find "the Committee for the Remonstrance to meet
between . . . and two clock. The Committee for Arms, and
Tonnage and Poundage to sit at two clock. Mr. Banks in
the Chair." [22]   And then on the same afternoon "Mr. Bankes
reporteth from the Committee for Tonnage and Poundage,
the draught of the Remonstrance.—*Engrossetur*"; also "the
Remonstrance to be dispatched between seven and eight." [23]
In view of this intended remonstrance the King the next day
prorogued Parliament "some few hours before I meant it."

So much we may learn from the *Journals*. We need not
pursue this bill further. If I deal at some length with a
matter which the reader may find somewhat tedious, my
purpose is to show that the Commons consistently pursued
the same tactics. They meant not to make any grant or to
make but a temporary grant. They had been long enough
at the question; to pretend it was time that they lacked was
absurd—was, indeed, hypocritical.[24]   Gardiner goes once
more astray. For he writes under June the 14th, "Under the
influence of the feeling provoked by the rejection of the
Remonstrance the Commons went into committee on the
Bill for the grant of tonnage and poundage which had been
brought in at the beginning of the session, but had been postponed on account of the pressure of other business." [25]
Again, "the Tonnage and Poundage Bill had been brought

[21] *Ibid.*, I, p. 918. Yet Buckingham had written to Coke under date
of the 28th May: "I doubt not in a few days the Bill of Subsidies will
be passed for there is now likely to be a happy agreement between the
King and his people" *(Coke MSS.,* I, p. 345). There never would be
such agreement. Of that would the Commons make sure.
[22] *C.J.,* I, p. 919.
[23] *Ibid.,* I, p. 919.
[24] See Nethersole's account of the matter in a letter to the Queen of
Bohemia; certain matters requiring time to settle, "they desired to pass
a temporary Act"; *State Papers Domestic,* 1628–9, p. 183.
[25] *History,* VI, p. 322. Is June the 14th the right date? All I find in
the *Journals* is this: "The other Committees, for the Goldsmiths, and
Tonnage and Poundage, and continuance of Statutes, deferred till
Monday, two clock in the afternoon" (I, p. 913).

in early in the session. From time to time it had been mentioned but, except a few words from Phelips, nothing had been said to give to it any sort of prominence." [26]

And now let the King himself speak on the history of tonnage and poundage. In Rushworth's *Collections* we find " His Majesty's Declaration to all his loving Subjects, of the Causes which moved him to dissolve the last Parliament, March 10, 1628." [27] From this statement consider the following : " The session thus ended, and the Parliament risen, that intended remonstrance gave us occasion to look into the business of tonnage and poundage. And therefore, though our necessities pleaded strongly for us ; yet we were not apt to strain that point too far, but resolved to guide our self by the practice of former ages, and examples of our most noble predecessors ; thinking those counsels best warranted, which the wisdom of former ages, concurring with the present occasions did approve ; and therefore gave order for a diligent search of records : upon which it was found, that although in the Parliament holden in the first year of the reign of King Edward the Fourth, the subsidy of tonnage and poundage was not granted unto that King, but was first granted unto him by Parliament in the third year of his reign ; yet the same was accounted and answered to that King, from the first day of his reign, all the first and second years of his reign, and until it was granted by Parliament. And that in the succeeding times of King Richard the Third, King Henry the Seventh, King Henry the Eighth, King Edward the Sixth, Queen Mary, and Queen Elizabeth, the subsidy of tonnage and poundage was not only enjoyed by every of those Kings and Queens, from the death of each of them deceasing, until it was granted by Parliament unto the successor ; but in all those times (being for the most part peaceable, and not burdened with like charges and necessities, as these modern times) the Parliament did most readily and cheerfully, in the beginning of every of those reigns, grant the same, as a thing most necessary for the guarding of the

[26] *History*, VI, p. 327.
[27] Otherwise, 1629.

seas, safety and defence of the realm, and supportation of the royal dignity.[28]   And in the time of our royal father of blessed memory, he enjoyed the same a full year, wanting very few days, before his Parliament began; and above a year before the Act of Parliament for the grant of it was passed: and yet when the Parliament was assembled, it was granted without difficulty.   And in our own time, we quietly received the same three years and more, expecting with patience, in several Parliaments, the like grant thereof, as had been made to so many of our predecessors; the House of Commons still professing, that multitude of other businesses, and not want of willingness on their part, had caused the settling thereof to be so long deferred.   And therefore finding so much reason and necessity, for the receiving of the ordinary duties in the custom-house, to concur with the practice of such a succession of Kings and Queens, famous for wisdom, justice, and government; and nothing to the contrary, but that intended remonstrance, hatched out of the passionate brains of a few particular persons; we thought it was so far from the wisdom and duty of a House of Parliament, as we could not think, that any moderate and discreet man, (upon composed thoughts, setting aside passion and distemper) could be against receiving of tonnage and poundage; especially since we do, and still must, pursue those ends, and undergo that charge, for which it was first granted to the Crown; it having been so long and constantly continued to our predecessors, as that in four several Acts of Parliament for the granting thereof to King Edward the Sixth, Queen Mary, Queen Elizabeth, and our blessed father,[29] it is in express terms mentioned, to have been had and enjoyed by the several Kings, named in those Acts, time out of mind, by authority of Parliament.   And therefore upon these reasons, we held it agreeable to our kingly honour, and necessary for the safety and good of our kingdom, to continue the receipt thereof, as so many of our predecessors had done." [30]

[28] The reader should note the last phrase.
[29] Rushworth has a full stop at "father," but this should, no doubt, be a comma. See *Bibliotheca Regia,* p. 400.
[30] Rushworth, Appendix, p. 3; *Bibliotheca Regia,* p. 398.

This clear, yet concise, declaration was never, I think, controverted. Historians, it seems, are at one in ignoring King Charles's own words, though they cannot be thus disregarded. They merit as careful attention as the evidence of Eliot and others and may come better out of the scrutiny.

One further point must be dealt with. I mentioned the intended remonstrance that was drawn and allowed by the Commons in the year 1628. Though pleading the same lack of time, though containing the same protestations of zeal, of affection, of loyalty, this paper yet makes one new claim: " Nevertheless, your loyal Commons in this Parliament, out of their especial zeal to your service, and especial regard of your pressing occasions "—and this, let the reader mark well, in the fourth year from Charles's accession and the third of his parliaments also—" have taken into their consideration, so to frame a grant of subsidy of tonnage and poundage to your Majesty, that both you might have been the better enabled for the defence of your realm, and your subjects, by being secure from all undue charges, be the more encouraged cheerfully to proceed in their course of trade; by the increase whereof your Majesty's profit, and likewise the strength of the kingdom would be very much augmented.

" But not being now able to accomplish this their desire, there is no course left unto them, without manifest breach of their duty, both to your Majesty and their country, save only to make this humble declaration, That the receiving of tonnage and poundage, and other impositions not granted by Parliament, is a breach of the fundamental liberties of this kingdom, and contrary to your Majesty's royal answer to the said Petition of Right." [31]

This impudent claim can, I think, be disposed of without much ado; even Gardiner can say nothing for it. So runs the Petition of Right: " They do therefore humbly pray your most excellent Majesty, that no man hereafter be compelled to make or yield any gift, loan, benevolence, tax, or such like charge without common consent by Act of Parlia-

[31] Rushworth, p. 630; *Bibliotheca Regia*, p. 390.

ment." [32] Not one of these words could be twisted to cover the customs as such. Tonnage and poundage were " subsidies." No one would think of applying " gift," " loan " or " benevolence " to them. Nor yet can we rightly suppose the word " tax " was intended to cover them. Used on occasions more loosely, it properly meant direct payments. The Commons, had they meant to include them, instead of " or such like charge " would have mentioned the tonnage and poundage or " the subsidy of tonnage and poundage." [33] Then, again, the King's words are explicit : " And then some glances in the House, but open rumours abroad were spread, that by the answer to the Petition, we had given away not only our impositions upon goods exported and imported, but the tonnage and poundage ; whereas in the debate and hammering of that Petition, there was no speech or mention in either House concerning those impositions ; but concerning taxes and other charges within the land : much less was there any thought thereby to debar us of tonnage and poundage ; which both before and after the answer to the Petition, the House of Commons in all their speeches and treaties did profess they were willing to grant." [34] So again, in proroguing the Houses, the King used the following terms :

" It may seem strange, that I come so suddenly to end this session. Therefore, before I give my assent to the bills, I will tell you the cause ; though I must avow, that I owe an account to none but to God alone. It is known to every one, that a while ago the House of Commons gave me a remonstrance ; how acceptable, every man may judge ; and, for the merit of it, I will not call that in question, for I am sure no wise man can justify it. Now since I am certainly informed, that a second remonstrance is preparing for me, to take away my

---

[32] Gardiner's *Constitutional Documents* (1906), p. 69.

[33] See " as if there might be any subsidy," p. 136, *supra.*

[34] *Bibliotheca Regia,* p. 397. Rushworth (Appendix, p. 2) makes non-sense of the opening sentence. We learn from some notes in the former that copies of this precious remonstrance were " scattered and dispersed abroad " " from one hand to another," the more to encourage the merchants in refusing the payment of the customs, which never before they refused " since the time of King Henry the Sixth," and that it was on this account that Charles published the declaration explaining at some length his motives for dissolving the third of his parliaments.

profit of tonnage and poundage (one of the chief maintenances of the Crown) by alleging, that I have given away
my right thereof, by my answer to your Petition; this is so
prejudicial unto me, that I am forced to end this session some
few hours before I meant it, being not willing to receive any
more remonstrances, to which I must give a harsh answer.

" And since I see, that even the House of Commons begins
already to make false constructions of what I granted in your
Petition, lest it be worse interpreted in the country, I will now
make a declaration concerning the true intent thereof. The
profession of both Houses, in the time of hammering this
Petition, was, in no ways to trench upon my prerogative;
saying, they had neither intention, nor power, to hurt it.
Therefore, it must needs be conceived, that I have granted no
new, but only confirmed the ancient, liberties of my subjects.
Yet, to show the clearness of my intentions, that I neither
repent, nor mean to recede from anything I have promised
you, I do here declare, that those things, which have been
done, whereby men had some cause to suspect the liberty of
the subjects to be trenched upon (which indeed was the first
and true ground of the Petition) shall not hereafter be drawn
into example to your prejudice; and, in time to come, in the
word of a King, you shall not have the like cause to complain.

" But as for tonnage and poundage, it is a thing I cannot
want; and was never intended by you to ask; never meant, I
am sure, by me to grant.

" To conclude, I command you all, that are here, to take
notice of what I have spoken at this time, to be the true
intent and meaning of what I have granted you in your
Petition; but especially you, my Lords the Judges; for to you
only, under me, belongs the interpretation of laws; for none
of the Houses of Parliament, joint or separate (what new
doctrine soever hath been raised) [have] any power, either to
make, or declare, a law, [without] my consent." [35]

[35] *Commons' Journals*, I, p. 919; *Bibliotheca Regia*, p. 328; Rushworth, p. 631. The *Bibliotheca* and Rushworth say "may" and not
"hath been raised." The *Lords' Journals*, however, as printed, read
"none of the House of Commons." I doubt that this makes any sense,
although Gardiner both cites and adopts it. See *L.J.*, III, p. 879;
History, VI, p. 325, and note 1.

CHAPTER VI

THE GREAT BREACH OF 1629

In January, 1629, the third parliament met once again. In the meantime it seems that some merchants, refusing the payment of the customs, had found their goods seized by the Crown and, among them, a member of parliament, known by the name of John Rolls. Their complaints were at once taken up. For, " a day "—here we quote the King's words —" being appointed to treat of the grant of tonnage and poundage : at the time prefixed all express great willingness to grant it. But a new strain is found out that it could not be done without great peril to the right of the subject, unless we should disclaim any right therein, but by grant in Parliament ; and should cause all those goods to be restored which upon commandment from us or our Counsel, were stayed by our officers until those duties were paid, and consequently should put our self out of possession of the tonnage and poundage before they were granted ; for else it was pretended the subject stood not in fit case to grant it ; a fancy and cavil raised of purpose to trouble the business : it being evident that all the Kings before named did receive that duty and were in actual possession of it, before and at the very time, when it was granted to them by Parliament. And although we to remove all difficulties, did from our own mouth, in those clear and open terms that might have satisfied, and well-disposed minds declare, that it was our meaning, by the gift of our people [1] to enjoy it, and that we did not challenge it of right, but took it *de bene esse,* showing thereby not the right but the necessity by which we had power to take it ; wherein we descended for their satisfaction, so far beneath our self, as we are confident never any of our predecessors did the like, nor was the like ever required or

---

[1] " Meaning " in the *Bibliotheca* is, no doubt, a printer's mistake. " People " should be read as in Rushworth, Appendix, p. 7.

expected from them; yet, for all this the bill of tonnage and poundage was laid aside, upon pretence [2] they must first clear the right of the subject therein, under colour whereof they entertain the complaints not only of John Rolls, a member of their House, but also of Richard Chambers, John Fowks, and Bartholomew Gilman against the officers of our customs, for detaining their goods upon refusal to pay the ordinary duty accustomed to be paid for the same." [3] This brings us at once to the *Journals.* We read on the 23rd January: "A message from his Majesty, by Mr. Secretary Cooke, for forbearance of any further debate about his officers' seizure of merchants' goods, till after to-morrow, two clock; at which time his Majesty intendeth to speak to both Houses, in the Banqueting-house at Whitehall." [4] Charles observed in the course of this speech: "The complaint I speak of is for staying men's goods, that denied tonnage and poundage; and this may have an easy and short conclusion (if my words and actions be rightly understood) for by passing the bill as mine ancestors have had it, my by-past actions will be included, and my future actions authorised; which certainly would not have been stuck upon, if men had not imagined, that I had taken this duty as appertaining to my hereditary prerogative. In which they are much deceived, for it ever was, and still is my meaning, by the gift of my people to enjoy it; and my intent in my speech at the end of the last session, was not to challenge tonnage and poundage as of right, but *de bene esse,* shewing you the necessity, not the right by which I was to take it, until I had it granted unto me, assuring my self (according to your general professions) that you wanted time not will to grant it unto me. Wherefore now having opportunity, I expect, that without loss of time you make good your professions, and so by passing the bill, to put an end to all questions arising from this subject, especially since I have

[2] "Patience" must be wrong in the text. "Pretence," as in Rushworth, seems right.

[3] *Bibliotheca Regia,* p. 405, in the King's Declaration of his reasons for dissolving the third of his parliaments. The King mentions also one Philips (p. 408).

[4] *Commons' Journals,* I, p. 921.

cleared all scruples that may trouble you in this business. To conclude, let us not be jealous of one another's actions, etc." [5] Go back in the light of this statement to the speech of the 26th June. " A second remonstrance," said the King, " is preparing for me, to take away my profit of tonnage and poundage (one of the chief maintenances of the Crown) by alleging, that I have given away my right thereof, by my answer to your Petition." Inasmuch as the Petition of Right had no bearing on tonnage and poundage, how then, by accepting that Petition, could Charles " give away " his rights in them ? And yet he lays no stress upon them. He continues : " This is so prejudicial unto me "—let the word " prejudicial " be noticed—" that I am forced to end this session some few hours before I meant it, being not willing to receive any more remonstrances, to which I must give a harsh answer. And since I see, that even the House of Commons begins already to make false constructions of what I granted in your Petition, lest it be worse interpreted in the country, I will now make a declaration concerning the true intent thereof. The profession of both Houses, in the time of hammering this Petition, was, no ways to trench upon my prerogative ; saying, they had neither intention, nor power, to hurt it. Therefore it must needs be conceived, that I have granted no new, but only confirmed the ancient, liberties of my subjects. Yet to show the clearness of my intentions, that I neither repent, nor mean to cede from anything I have promised you, I do here declare, that those things, which have been done, whereby men had some cause to suspect the liberty of the subjects to be trenched upon (which indeed was the first and true ground of the Petition) shall not hereafter be drawn into example to your prejudice ; and, in time to come, in the word of a King, you shall not have the like cause to complain. But as for tonnage and poundage, it is a thing I cannot want ; and was never intended by you to ask ; never meant, I am sure, by me to grant." [6]   " But as for," I think,

<hr />

[5] *Bibliotheca Regia*, p. 331 ; Rushworth, p. 664. This speech is mentioned in the *Journals* as read to the House by the Speaker, but nothing is said of its contents (I, p. 922).

[6] *Commons' Journals*, I, p. 919 ; see p. 144, *supra*.

shows that Charles here distinguishes tonnage and poundage from taxes, benevolences, loans, and, I take it, " to want " in this context has the meaning of being without. " I cannot," that is, " be without it," or, as we say now, " do without it." [7] " Never intended by you to ask; never meant, I am sure, by me to grant." These phrases bear on the Petition but suffer from too great conciseness. I take them to mean that the Commons in framing the Petition of Right can have had no intention whatever of including the tonnage and poundage and Charles no intention in his answer of yielding his rights in those levies.[8] These words may, perhaps, have occasioned some genuine misunderstanding, if actually spoken as stated. We know, none the less, that their curtness could well be excused in the circumstance.[9]

The following passage in Rushworth appears to bear on the main questions : " The meeting of the Parliament now drawing nigh [in the year 1629], the King consults with a select committee of his Privy Councillors, what probably the Parliament at their next meeting would insist upon, and how the Privy Council (who are members of the Parliament) shall demean themselves in such cases : and first it was proposed to his Majesty's consideration, that if in the House of Commons it shall be moved with any strength that the merchants' goods be delivered, before they proceed to the Bill of Tonnage and Poundage, the answer by such as are Privy Councillors and members of the House to be, that if the House intend to grant tonnage and poundage to the King, as it hath been granted to his predecessors, it will end all dispute ; but if they proceed otherwise then, before they come to a resolution, the King to speak to them, and to declare, that though his predecessors claimed it not but by grant of Parliament, yet took it *de facto,* until it was granted by Parliament, and that his Majesty hath done the like, and that if they will pass

---

[7] So Hacket, I think, understood it : " They knew he could not want this Stock, as well to guard the Kingdom as to support his own Dignity " (*Scrinia Reserata,* II, p. 83).

[8] See Hacket again : " To go further it was not his Meaning nor their Demand " (*ibid.,* II, p. 80).

[9] Provided, I mean, Charles's statements are given by the *Journals* verbatim.

the bill to his Majesty, as his ancestors had it, his Majesty will do any reasonable thing, to declare that he claims not tonnage and poundage otherwise than by grant in Parliament; but if this do not satisfy, then to avow a breach upon just cause given, not sought by the King.   And for bringing the King's business to a speedy issue, it was advised, that the Bill of Tonnage and Poundage be prepared before the Parliament sit, in the same form as it passed to King James, adding words to give it from the first day of the King's reign, and that the bill be presented at the first sitting of the Parliament, and the Privy Council of the House to declare that his Majesty caused it to be timely presented, to cut off all questions and debates, and to persuade them to a dispatch thereof, and that they will return a speedy answer whether they will grant tonnage and poundage or not." [10]   So great was the patience of Charles, notwithstanding delays and intrigues now extending to nearly four years.

" The session," he said at Whitehall, " beginning with confidence one towards the other, it may end with a perfect good understanding, which God grant."   But how did the Commons respond?   This the following entry shows clearly :

" A message from his Majesty, concerning the speeding of the Bill of Tonnage and Poundage.

Resolved, A Committee, to pen an answer herein to his Majesty.

1.   Head, the inconvenience arising by these messages, by debate and loss of time.

2.   Head, thanks to his Majesty for his care for religion.

3.   That the matter of tonnage and poundage arising naturally from this House, we resolve, in fit time, to take a course in it, as we hope, to his Majesty's satisfaction.

4.   That we intend not to dispute any the novel opinions; but, that the course, we will take, shall tend to his Majesty's honour.

[10] Rushworth, p. 642.   There seems no good reason for doubting that something like this is correct.   The bill was presented by Coke, we are told on p. 653 : " He said his Majesty much desired it, but it was a mistake that his Majesty commanded it."   There is nothing of this in the *Journals*.   See a letter from May, " ill in bed," to Sir J. Coke in *Coke MSS.,* " sends Bill for Tonnage and Poundage to be offered to the House " (I, p. 381).   The printed report must be wrong in assigning this letter to " February."

Mr Secretary Cooke, Sir Nath. Rich, Sir W. Earle, Sir D. Digges, Sir Jo. Ellyott, Mr Selden, to go presently about it, in the Treasury Chamber in the Exchequer : none there to trouble them." [11]

The men who could draw up those heads and appeal to " the inconvenience arising by these messages, by debate and loss of time," while protesting that " in fit time " they " would take a course " that " should tend to his Majesty's honour," must have been without all sense of shame—to say nothing of all sense of humour. The House soon agreed on its answer; the King named a time to receive it. [12] It followed the lines indicated and gave to religion " precedency." It went somewhat further, however, asserting that " the manner of possessing the House therewith " was " disagreeable to our orders and privileges, that we could not proceed therein." [13]

The King in his answer observed in regard to this matter of privilege : " I cannot think, that whereas you allege, that the Bill of Tonnage and Poundage was brought in against the privilege of your House, that you will offer to take so much privilege from any one of your members, as not to allow them the liberty to bring them in any bill whatsoever, though it be in your power when it is brought in, to do with it what you think good. And I cannot imagine how coming hither only by my power, and to treat of things I propound unto [you], you can deny me that prerogative to recommend or

[11] *Commons' Journals*, I, p. 923, January 28.

[12] *Ibid.*, I, pp. 924, 925.

[13] Rushworth, p. 651. As I said on an earlier page, I suspect these appeals to " religion " had never deceived the young King. In this context " His Majesty's answer, January 31 [1628–9], to the petition of both Houses for a public fast " should be much better known than it is for its humour as well as its shrewdness. " The chiefest motive," he said, " of your fast being the deplorable estate of the Reformed Churches abroad is too true, and our duties are (so much as in us possibly lieth) to give them help ; but certainly fighting will do them more good than fasting ; though I do not wholly disallow the latter, yet I must tell you, that this custom of fasts every session is but lately begun, and I confess I am not so fully satisfied with the necessity of it at this time, yet to show you how smoothly I desire our business to go on, eschewing (as much as I can) questions and jealousies, I do willingly grant your request herein. But with this note, that I expect that this shall not hereafter be brought into precedent for frequent fasts, except upon great occasions. As for the form and time, I will advise with my Lords the Bishops, and then send you a particular to both Houses " (*Bibliotheca Regia*, p. 333).

offer any bill unto you, though in this particular I must profess that this bill was not to have been offered you in my
name, as that member of your House [Sir John Coke] can
bear me witness." "As for Tonnage and Poundage," said
the King, "I do not desire it out of greediness (being persuaded you will make no stop in it when you take it in hand)
as out of a desire to put an end to all questions that daily
arise between me, and some of my subjects, thinking it a
strange thing if you should give ear unto those complaints,
and not take the sure and speedy way to decide them." In
regard to the pleas of the Commons that religion delayed his
own business, the King very shrewdly remarked : "I must
think it strange that this business of religion should be only a
hinderer of my affairs, whereas I am certainly informed that
all other things go on according to their ordinary course,
therefore I must still be instant with you, that you proceed
with this business of tonnage and poundage with diligence,
not looking to be denied in so just a desire, and you must not
think it much if I finding you slack shall give you such further
quickening as I find cause." [14]

This answer was read in the Commons on the following
morning by Coke ;[15] but no bill for the grant of the customs
seems even to have had a first reading.

They fell to at length—in a fashion.[16] And now were
strange courses adopted, anarchic, subversive of law, under-
mining all authority and order. The farmers were sent for
and questioned and ordered to bring out the warrants on
which they collected the duties and were kept for a whole
month together, day in and day out, in attendance. Mes-
sengers hastened to Heath to demand that he render account
of some orders the King himself issued. Not even the judges
escaped. Some were sent to examine them also, albeit they
owed to the House no account of judicial proceedings. A
" captious," " directory message " was sent to the Court of
Exchequer. The merchants petitioned the Commons; the

[14] *Bibliotheca Regia*, p. 334 ; Rushworth, p. 652.
[15] *Commons' Journals*, I, p. 926.
[16] From this point I take the main facts from *Bibliotheca Regia*,
pp. 406–13.

merchants, said the Commons, should have privilege. No Court should grant out an attachment. A letter should be sent the Lord Keeper, as though it were thus in their power to control the Law Courts at Westminster. This letter did not reach the Keeper. Wild language was used by the " Country " —the King's " wicked counsels " and so on—but passed without censure or check. Then they summoned the Sheriff of London and questioned him, too, in a matter outside of their own jurisdiction. But, failing to get such an answer as suited their particular purpose, they sent him forthwith to the Tower.

" Lastly," the King himself tells us, " in their proceedings against our customers, they went about to censure them as delinquents, and to punish them for staying some goods of some factious merchants in our store-house, for not paying those duties which themselves had formerly paid, and which the customers without interruption, had received of all other merchants many years before, and to which they were authorized both by our great seal, and by several directions and commandments from us and our Privy Council. To give some colour to their proceedings herein, they went about to create a new privilege which we will never admit; that a parliament man hath privilege for his goods against the King, the consequence whereof will be, that he may not be constrained to pay any duties to the King during the time of privilege of Parliament. It is true, they would have made this case to have been between the merchants and our farmers of our customs, and have severed them from our interest and commandment, thereby the rather to make them liable to the censure and punishment of that House. But on the other side, we holding it both unjust and dishonourable to withdraw our self from our officers in anything they did by our commandment, or disavow anything which we had enjoined to be done; upon Monday the 23 of February sent a message unto them by Secretary Coke, thanking them for the respect they had showed in severing the interest of our farmers from our own interest and commandment; nevertheless we were bound in honour to acknowledge a truth, and what was done by them, was done by our express direction and commandment, and if for doing thereof our farmers should suffer, it would highly concern us in honour : which message was no sooner delivered unto them, but in a tumultuous and discontented manner, they called, *Adjourn, Adjourn,* and thereupon, without any cause given on our part, in a very unusual manner, adjourned themselves until the Wednesday following; on which day, by the uniform advice of our Privy Council, we caused both Houses to be adjourned until the second day of March, hoping that in the meantime a better and more right understanding might be begotten between us and the members of that House, whereby the Parliament might come to a happy issue. But understanding by a good advertisement, that their discontent did not in that time digest and pass away, we resolved to make a second adjournment until the tenth of March; which was done as well to take time to our self, to think of some means to accommodate those difficulties, as to give them time to advise better; and accordingly we gave commandment for a second adjournment in both Houses, and for cessation of all business till the day appointed." [17]   The Lords' House obeyed the command; but on Finch's delivering the message, he found it " straightways contradicted." Citing numerous precedents, therefore, he reminded the House that the King had an absolute power to adjourn and not only to prorogue or dissolve. But members sprang up on all sides and declared they had business to do— till that business was done, no adjournment. The Speaker, repeating the message, declared he would now leave the Chamber, reporting at once to the King in obedience to Charles's command. Holles, however, and Valentine held him perforce in his seat, till at length he found means to get out, whereupon they and others seized on him and thrust him back into the Chair. Then Eliot, flourishing a paper, called out that the Speaker should read it. The Speaker refusing to read it, he thereupon read it himself and loudly demanded of Finch that he put it at once to the House. The Speaker, refusing this also, was bitterly assailed by " the Country," and

[17] *Bibliotheca Regia,* p. 410.

covered with " taunts and invectives." [18]   Then Charles himself sent for the Sergeant, one Grimston; the Commons detained him.   The door was immediately locked, and the keys he had taken from Grimston were safe in Sir Miles Hobart's pocket.   No courtier should go to the King.   All was tumult, disorder and violence, blows struck on the floor of the House and men's hands on the hilts of their swords.   New times and " new counsels," new manners!   Charles summoned the Gentleman Usher and sent him across with a message.   The Commons refused him admission.   But Eliot's voice could at times be heard rising above all the tumult. Then Holles stood forth, a sham Speaker, to put then and there certain motions.   The first had to do with " religion " (" religion " " preceding," as usual), two others with tonnage and poundage, embodied in terms such as these: " Whosoever shall counsel or advise the taking and levying of the subsidies of tonnage and poundage, not being granted by Parliament, or shall be an actor or instrument therein, shall be likewise reputed an innovator in the government, and a capital enemy to the kingdom and commonwealth ; " [19]   " If any merchant or person whatsoever shall voluntarily yield, or pay the said subsidies of tonnage and poundage, not being granted by Parliament, he shall likewise be reputed a betrayer of the liberties of England, and an enemy to the same."   Thus did Holles declaim to the House, while his friends at each pause roared approval.   So Charles was " a capital enemy," unless he consented to starve.   If they could, they would put him to death.   That was what the word " capital " meant. Then at last by adjourning themselves, still refusing to hear the King's message, they flung the doors wide and burst forth.[20]

---

[18] The reader should note that to these men not even the Speaker was inviolable.   Nothing should stand in their way, could they compass the ruin of the monarchy.

[19] " To the kingdom " and not " to the King."   Note this subtle and ingenious distinction.   These men were themselves the " innovators."

[20] For March 2 the *Journals* have only: " Mr. Speaker delivereth a message from his Majesty.   Mr. Speaker, in the name of the House, adjourneth it till to-morrow sevennight, nine clock " (I, p. 932).   The

To starve or dissolve thus the issue, Charles now had no choice but the latter. And so for a decade and more he ruled wisely and well without Parliament.[21]

NOTE

In regard to these earlier parliaments Clarendon has this remark, which, indeed, is as cryptic as curt: "Thus, after the death of King James, his majesty received it [the tonnage and poundage], till the first parliament was summoned; and, that and two more being unfortunately dissolved, (as was said before,) in which his ministers were not solicitous enough for the passing that act for tonnage and poundage, continued the receipt of it till this [the Long] parliament" (see his *History* [1849], I, pp. 369ff.). I can find no support for this statement apart from the claim made by Williams, nor can I find aught to refute it. But Charles was "solicitous" enough—we have seen—in the last of these sessions, and the Commons pretended that his messages caused "loss of time" and "inconveniences." Further, we are driven to ask "What did Clarendon mean by 'that act'?" For the context, it seems, makes it clear that "that act" for the tonnage and poundage means a bill in the customary form, not a temporary bill such as Williams had taken the credit of "staying" and ministers might well, indeed, be but little disposed to "solicit."

This brings us again to the question: had Clarendon any real knowledge? He writes as though all was plain sailing

principal facts are well known, and some details are not of great moment. The motions propounded by Holles are given as stated by Rushworth (p. 660). They are given in Forster's biography in almost identical terms (*Sir John Eliot*, II, p. 457).

[21] When at last the Long Parliament carried a bill for the tonnage and poundage, the grant was "for two months only, in which time a new book of rates should be made, more advantageous to his Majesty in point of profit" ("which was always," says Clarendon, "solemnly professed") "and then a complete act might pass." Still the same disingenuous tactics! The plot was at last working well. See Clarendon, *History of the Rebellion and Civil Wars in England* (1849), I, pp. 370–1. "Two months" should be, strictly speaking, "from the five and twentieth of May, one thousand six hundred forty-one, to the fifteenth of July next ensuing" (Gardiner's *Constitutional Documents*, p. 161).

and the Commons would have voted the customs for life in traditional form, had the King or his servants insisted. One bill alone passed through the Commons; the grant was for one year alone. Did he know or not know of that fact? If he knew it, it should have been mentioned, as essential to any sound statement of "the truth," as he calls it, "of the case." I suspect he did not know the truth. He was only a boy of seventeen, when the young King ascended the throne. "I am not altogether a stranger," he writes, "to the passages of those parliaments, (though I was not a member of them,) having carefully perused the journals of both houses, and familiarly conversed with many who had principal parts in them." [22] But no student, however acute, could have learnt from the *Journals* what passed in the matter of tonnage and poundage in the year 1625. As for those "who had principal parts," they can hardly have told him the truth. Otherwise, why suppress it years later—and that in a work not intended, it seems, for the eyes of the public? Of what some of those may have told him we can, perhaps, form some idea from the fictions recorded by Eliot. Remembering, moreover, that later he sided at first with the Commons, which proved him indifferent or blind to the fundamental questions at issue, I repeat that we cannot rely on his statements for these early years.

---

[22] *History,* I, p. 6.

CHAPTER VII

A LETTER addressed to the King in the earlier days of his reign and preserved with the rest of his papers deserves to be cited in full and examined with care by the student. The writer is not, I think, known, nor, indeed, does it bear any date. But the date within limits is clear. " May it please his most excellent Majesty to consider, that this great opposition against the Duke of Buckingham is stirred up and maintained by such who either maliciously or ignorantly and concurrently seek the debasing of this free Monarchy, which because they find not yet ripe to attempt against the King himself, they endeavour it against the Duke's side. These men though agreeing in one mischief, yet are of divers sorts and humours, viz.,

" 1. Meddling and busy persons, who took their first hint at the beginning of King James, when the Union was treated of in Parliament. That learned King gave too much way to those popular speeches, by the frequent proof he had of his great abilities in that kind.

" Since the time of Hen. 6. these parliamentary discoursings were never suffered, as being the certain symptoms of subsequent rebellions, civil wars and the dethroning of our Kings. But these last twenty years, most of the Parliament men seek to improve the reputation of their wisdoms by their declamations, and no honest patriot dare oppose them, lest he incur the reputation of a fool, or a coward in his country's cause.

" 2. Covetous landlords, enclosers, depopulators, and justices of the peace, who have got an habit of omniregency, and an hope to extend the same against the King in Parliament, as they do on his subjects in the country. Hereby the King loseth £24,000 in every whole subsidy, for *anno* 1600 it was £80,000, and now it is but £56,000, which cometh by

157

the decay of yeomanry, who were three and four pound men. And these gentlemen (most of them of the Parliament) do ease themselves to afflict those who are the true commons, and yet persuade them that the grievances are caused by the Duke, and the ill government of the King.

" 3. Recusants and Church-Papists, whose hatred is irreconcilable against the Duke, for the breach of the Spanish match. The French lady, though as zealous a Catholic, does not please them, for they were tied to Spain by their hopes of a change of religion that way. All the priests are sent from the Spanish dominions, and the sons and daughters of the Papists remain as hostages of their fidelities in the colleges and nunneries of the King of Spain. And though the Papists have no place in the House of Commons, yet privately they aggravate all scandals against the Duke, to kindle a separation against the King and his people, and avert them from enabling the King to resist, or be avenged of our great enemy. Remember the course held by these men in the Parliament of Undertakers. Also Doctor Egbesham and all the priests daily practice, libelling against all great men about the King.

" 4. Needy and indebted persons in both Houses, who endeavour by these parliamentary stirs, not so much the Duke's overthrow, as a rebellion, which they hope will follow, if it be not done. This is much to be suspected, as well by their calumniations against his Majesty, as for their own wants; many of them being outlawed, and not able to show their heads but in Parliament time by privilege thereof, and they know that there are enough to follow them in the same mischief.

" 5. Puritans and all other sectaries, who though scarce two of them agree in what they would have, yet they all in general are haters of government. They began in Parliament about *anno* 23 Eliz. and spit their venom not only against the Bishops, but also against the Lord Chancellor Hatton, and others, the Queen's favourites, and counsellors, as they do now against the clergy and the Duke. But their main discontentment is against the King's government, which they

would have extinguished in matters ecclesiastical, and limited
in temporal. This is a fearful and important consideration,
because it pretends conscience and religion, and they now
more deadly hate the Duke, because he showeth himself to
be no Puritan, as they hoped he would at his return from
Spain.

"6. Malcontents censured or decourted for their deserts,
as the kindred and dependants of the Earl of Suffolk, and of
Sir Henry Yelverton, Cook, Lake, Middlesex, though all of
them (the last excepted) were dejected by King James,
without any concurrency of the Duke; others because they
are not preferred, as they imagine that they deserve, as the
Lord Say, Earl of Clare, Sir John Eliot, Selden, and Glanvil,
Sir Dudley Digs, and the Bishops of Norwich and Lincoln.
These and many others according to the nature of envy look
upon everyone with an evil eye, especially upon the Duke,
who either hath or doth not prefer them to those places, or
retain them in them, which their ambition expecteth.

"7. Lawyers in general, for that (as Sir Edward Cook
could not but often express) our Kings have upholden the
power of their prerogatives, and the rights of their clergy,
whereby their comings in have been abated. And therefore
the lawyers are fit ever in Parliaments to second any complaint against both Church and King, and all his servants,
with their cases, antiquities, records, statutes, precedents, and
stories. But they cannot, or will not call to mind, that never
any nobleman in favour with his sovereign was questioned in
Parliament, except by the King himself in case of treason, or
unless it were in the nonage and tumultuous times of Rich. 2.
Hen. 6. or Edw. 6. which happened to the destruction both of
the King and kingdom. And that not to exceed our own and
fathers' memories, in King Hen. 8. time, Woolsey's exorbitant
power and pride, and Cromwell's contempt of the nobility,
and the laws, were not yet permitted to be discussed in Parliament, though they were most odious and grievous to all the
kingdom. And that Leicester's undeserved favour and faults,
Hatton's insufficiency, and Rawleigh's insolence far exceeded
what yet hath been (though most falsely) objected against the

Duke : yet no lawyer durst abet, nor any man else begin any invectives against them in Parliament.

" 8. The merchants and citizens of London, convinced (not by the Duke, but by Cranfield and Ingram) to have deceived the King of imposts and customs, and deservedly fearing to be called to an account for undoing all the other cities and good towns, and the poor colony of Virginia, as also for the transportation of our silver into the East Indies; these vent their malice upon the Duke in the Exchange, Paul's, Westminster-Hall, with their suggestions, and therein they wound both to subjects and strangers, the honour of his Majesty and his proceedings.

" 9. Innovators, *plebicolae,* and King-haters. At the latter end of Queen Elizabeth, it was a phrase to speak, yea for to pray for the Queen and State. This word ' State,' was learned by our neighbourhood and commerce with the Low-Countreys, as if we were, or affected to be governed by States. This the Queen saw and hated. And the old Earl of Oxford his propositions at her death, they awakened King James to prevent this humour, and to oppose the conditions and limitations presented unto him by the Parliament.

" The lawyers, citizens, and Western men (who are most hot infected with Puritanism) stood strong against him under a colour of Parliaments, and parliamentary privileges. His Majesty therefore strengthened himself ever with some favourite, as whom he might better trust, than many of the nobility tainted with this desire of oligarchy. It behoveth without doubt his Majesty to uphold the corner-stone, on which the demolishing of his monarchy will be builded. For if they prevail with this, they have hatched a thousand other demands to pull the feathers of the Royalty, they will appoint him servants, counsellors, alliances, limits of his expense, accounts of his revenues, chiefly if they can (as they mainly desire) they will now dazzle him in the beginning of his reign.

" 10. King James and King Charles lastly are the Duke's accusers (my meaning is, with all humble reverence to their honours and memories, and to speak in the sense of the House of Commons) both their Majesties are *coniuncta*

persona,[1] in all the aspersions which are laid upon the Duke.
For instance, the Parliament's money destined for the wars,
spent in the treaties, messages, ambassadors, and entertainment of the King's marriage, and the burial of his father, and
the war in the name of the Count Palatine, the breach of
both the treaties which then canonized the Duke, but now is
made evidence against him; the honours and offices con-
ferred upon him by King James, that his Majesty might with
his own counsel direct their managing, the setting forth of
the navy, though to the Duke's great charge, by both their
commandments; the match with France, and whatsoever
generally hath not been successful to men's expectations. All
these, though the acts of the Kings, are imputed to the Duke,
who, if he suffer for obeying his sovereigns, the next attempt
will be to call the King to account for anything he under-
takes, which doth not prosperously succeed, as all men would
have it.

"If it please his Majesty to remove and set aside all these
disadvantages, he shall find the charge laid against the Duke
will prove very empty, and all of small moment. And for
them, if his Majesty and the Duke's Grace think it no im-
peachment to their honours, all that the Parliament hath
objected against the Duke, is pardoned at the King's coronation, which benefit every poor subject enjoyeth, three things
only excepted, which may most easily be answered." [2]

Comprehensive, indeed, is this paper, in what way soever
you take it—as history, conjecture or indictment. Its author
has grasp, breadth of vision. His style is both clear and concise and his mind bent on facts, not on phrases, and void of
both sentiment and rhetoric. Moreover, he claims to know well
what designs were in secret afoot. He cannot be set aside
lightly. A paper preserved with such care must have had
very solid foundations.

The King himself apparently detected the hand of the
Jesuits also. "And observing the subtilty," he remarked, "of

---

[1] Or *coniunctae personae?*
[2] *Bibliotheca Regia,* p. 286. There is a full stop at "enjoyeth" in the
last sentence.

M

the adverse party, he cannot but believe that the hand of Joab hath been in this disaster, that the common Incendiaries of Christendom have subtilly and secretly insinuated these things which unhappily (and, as his Majesty hopeth, beyond the inventions of the Actors) have caused these diversions and distractions." [3]

I presume that the Jesuits are meant, for we find in a Commons' petition of December 3, 1621, the same language applied to the Jesuits—"The swarms of priests and Jesuits, the common incendiaries of all Christendom, dispersed in all parts of your kingdom." [4] The coincidence, at least, is very striking. If not, whom had Charles in his mind and how else would his readers understand him? It is difficult now to determine what warrant there was for this charge. But I think it must have had a solid basis, being publicly made to the nation.

There are curious suggestions, I may add, of more underground forces at work in the letters and papers of the period, and more in the period that followed—Rosicrucians, Freemasons and Brownists, Anabaptists, Independents and Levellers, atheists and Jews. Some, at least, of these casual suggestions have been noted by Isaac Disraeli; and they merit a more thorough inquiry than as yet I have been able to give them.

The King himself ascribed the Civil War in a number of statements still existing to some of the factions just mentioned; and he spoke on occasion as though he suspected some still deeper plot, some more sinister and secret force at work. There is also a curious passage in the speech that he made on the scaffold, that historians have quite overlooked. A new field of inquiry thus is opened, that may finally expose the prime movers.

I would recommend readers who can get it to read Walker's

---

[3] " His Majestie's Declaration concerning the Causes of his dissolving the two first Parliaments of his Reign, *Anno* 1625, 1626 "; *Bibliotheca Regia*, p. 365.

[4] G. W. Prothero, *Statutes and Constitutional Documents, 1558–1625*, p. 308.

book on Independency, a scathing indictment of Cromwell and the men who had murdered their King and the men who stuffed loot in their pockets.   This Walker was no Cavalier. " What a crew ! " you will probably say.[5]

[5] Clement Walker, *The Complete History of Independency* (1661).

CHAPTER VIII

EPILOGUE

WE raised at the outset these questions, " Which side was it opened hostilities? Which declared war on the other? " The answer we found in the history of Charles's first parliament in London. Rejecting the offer Heath made and refusing Charles tonnage and poundage for more than a year at a time, they adopted revolutionary courses or what they themselves called " new counsels." They showed their hand only too plainly. They struck at the King and the monarchy. Both could be starved by such measures and either in due course abolished or reduced to an abject surrender. This point is as clear as can be and is fully borne out by what followed in the next and in subsequent years. It was not the King's servants they aimed at. Such tactics had little to do with that lack, which the Commons pretended, of confidence in the great Duke. They, moreover, evaded throughout all their pledges regarding the war they themselves used the King to bring on. Let me quote here some words of the King: " I must withal put you in mind of times past; you may remember my father moved by your counsel, and won by your persuasions, brake the treaties; in these persuasions I was your instrument towards him, and I was glad to be instrumental in anything which might please the whole body of the realm : nor was there any then in greater favour with you than this man, whom you now so traduce. And now when you find me so sure entangled in war, as I have no honourable and safe retreat, you make my necessity your privilege, and set what rate you please upon your supplies; a practice not very obliging towards Kings. Mr. Cook told you, *It was better die by a foreign enemy, than be destroyed at home.* Indeed I think it is more honourable for a King to be invaded, and almost destroyed by a foreign enemy, than to be despised at home." [1] The King was, no doubt, well aware of the Commons' designs on himself. When in March, 1626, in an interview Totness begged Charles to regard his own ends and nought else, let the Council of War go to prison and suffer the Commons' displeasure—better so than to lose their supplies or to breed some unhappy distaste that must touch on his Majesty's person—" Let them do what they list," said the King; " you shall not go to the Tower. It is not you they aim at, but it is me upon whom they make inquisition; and for subsidies, that will not hinder it. Gold may be bought too dear, and I thank you for your offer." [2] That the Commons were aiming at Charles, not at Buckingham, also seems clear from the fact that upon the Duke's death they intensified all their attacks. The King himself noted this fact. We may quote his own words to his people : " Whilst the Duke of Buckingham lived, he was entitled to all the distempers and ill events of former Parliaments; and therefore much endeavour was used to demolish him, as the only wall of separation between us and our people. But now he is dead, no alteration was found amongst those envenomed spirits, which troubled then the blessed harmony between us and our subjects, and continue still to trouble it. For now under the pretence of public care of the commonwealth they suggest new and causeless fears, which in their own hearts they know to be false; and devise new engines of mischief, so to cast a blindness on the good affections of our people, that they may not see the truth, and largeness of our heart towards them : so that now it is manifest the Duke was not alone the mark that those men shot at, but was only as a mere Minister of ours taken upon the by, and in the passage to their more secret designs, which only were to cast our affairs into a desperate condition, to abate the powers of the Crown, and to bring our government into obloquy; that in

[1] *Bibliotheca Regia*, p. 285. This Coke was a son of Sir Edward. The message, itself bears no date but refers to March, 1626.
[2] *State Papers Domestic*, 1625, 1626, p. 275 ; March 9.

the end all things may be overwhelmed with anarchy and confusion." [3] How keenly the King diagnosed! For the end, as he said, would be anarchy, and time would at last prove his wisdom.

[3] *Bibliotheca Regia*, p. 414.

FIRST APPENDIX

THE King's speech at the opening of parliament gives rise to some curious questions. What did the King say exactly? I cited the little known version contained in the *Bibliotheca*.[1] This differs in language and substance from the version contained in the *Journals*, which Rushworth has almost repeated and may, for that matter, have copied.[2]

The speech, it seems certain, was short. For Williams, who followed, observed: "You have heard his Majesty's speech, though short, yet full and princely, and rightly imperatorious, as Tacitus said of Galba's: neither must we account that speaker to be short, *qui materiae immoratur*, that keeps himself close unto his theme, and subject. For as Pliny made his censure of Homer and Virgil, *Brevis uterque est, sed facit quod instituit*: either of them seem to be short, for they do their work so succinctly, there falls not a word besides the purpose. His Majesty hath himself abundantly expressed the substance, of what he offers to your consideration at this meeting."[3] Such language would hardly apply to the version contained in the *Journals*. Though "short," it is not, I think, "full" nor yet "princely" nor "imperatorious." It hardly "expresses the substance," as Williams would have it, "*abundantly*." Nothing, for instance, is said of the famous address from the Houses—*fons et origo* of all that was then taking place in those Houses. That Charles would, however, appeal to it—Buckingham did so at Oxford—is what we might fairly suppose. The description seems far more in

---

[1] *Bibliotheca Regia* (1659), p. 273.
[2] *Lords' Journals*, III, p. 435; Rushworth, p. 171.
[3] *Scrinia Reserata*, II, p. 9. This passage is not in the *Journals*. The last phrase is amply confirmed by the writer of the *Fawsley Debates* (p. 1). That "the King's speech was short" we know also from Chamberlain's letter to Carleton; see *Court and Times of Charles the First* (1848), I, p. 36.

keeping with the copy in the *Bibliotheca,* which also contains certain phrases so good that they seem to ring true. " And no breach of privilege neither " can hardly be someone's invention. The version that is given in the *Journals* has practically nothing in common with that in the *Bibliotheca* but the reference at the end to Gamaliel. Besides, it is very much vaguer, less pointed, less epigrammatic. All the versions are presumably summaries or simply a series of extracts. The writer of the *Fawsley Debates* will afford us, I fear, little help; his report is contained in twelve lines, which in all comprise only one sentence and bear no resemblance at all to the *Bibliotheca's* own version, though some to the copy in the *Journals,* since " our matchless fidelity and love to our king (the ancient honour of this nation) " finds a parallel in the latter in " the love and the fidelity you have ever borne to your Kings."

I venture to submit that the version I quoted comes nearest the truth, if we seek the *main points* of the speech. We know that a number of versions, some very imperfect and short, had been put into print at the time.[4] Where the editor, whoever he was, of the *Bibliotheca Regia* came by this little known copy we cannot now very well say. But he must have had access to records preserved on the royalist side. His collection is " semi-official." He gives, too, a number of speeches not elsewhere, I fancy, preserved.

Let me add the report in the *Journals,* that the reader may form his own judgement :

" The King's Majesty being placed in his royal throne, the Lords in their robes, and the Commons present below the bar, his Majesty commanded prayers to be said. And, during the time of prayers, his Majesty put off his crown, and kneeled by the chair of estate.

" Then it pleased his Majesty to declare the cause of the summons of this Parliament, in manner following : *videlicet,*

' My Lords Spiritual and Temporal, and you Gentlemen of the House of Commons, in this present Parliament assembled,

[4] See *Scrinia Reserata,* II, p. 9 ; Mead to Stuteville in *Court and Times,* I, p. 37.

' I thank God, that the business that is to be treated of at this time, is of such a nature that it needs no eloquence for to set it forth; for I am neither able to do it, nor doth it stand with my nature to spend much time in words. It is no new business (being already happily begun by my father of blessed memory that is with God); therefore it needs no narrative.

' I hope in God that you will go on to maintain it as freely as you were willing to advise my father to it. It is true, that it may seem to some that he was too slack to begin so just and so glorious a work; but it was his wisdom that made him loth to begin a work until he might find means to maintain it; but, after he saw how much he was abused in the confidence he had in other States, and was confirmed by your advices to run the course we are in, with your enagements to the maintaining of it; I need not press to prove how willingly he took your advice; for the preparations that are made are better able to declare it, than I can speak it; the assistance of those in Germany, the fleet that is ready for action, with the rest of the preparations, which I have only followed my father in, do sufficiently prove, that he entered not superficially, but really and heartily, into this action.

' My Lords and Gentlemen, I hope that you do remember, that you were pleased to employ me to advise my father, to break both those treaties that were then on foot, so that I cannot say that I came hither a free unengaged man. It is true, that I came into this business willingly, freely, like a young man, and consequently rashly; but it was by your entreaties, your engagements; so that, though it were done like a young man, yet I cannot repent me of it: and I think none can blame me for it, knowing the love and the fidelity you have ever borne to your Kings; I having had likewise some little experience of your affections. I pray you remember that, this being my first action, and begun by your advice and entreaty, what a great dishonour it were, both to you and me, if this action, so begun, should fail for that assistance you are able to give me; yet, knowing the constancy of your loves both to me and this business, I needed not to have said this, but only to shew what care and sense I have of your honours and mine own.

'I must entreat you likewise to consider of the times we are in; how that I must venture your lives, which I would be loth to do, if I should continue you here long; and you must venture the business, if you be slow in your resolutions; wherefore I hope you will take such grave and wise counsel, as you will expedite what you have now in hand to do, which will do me and yourselves an infinite deal of honour; you, in shewing your loves to me; and me, that I may perfect a work, which my father has so happily begun.

'Last of all, because some malicious men may, and as I hear have given out, that I am not so true a keeper and maintainer of the true religion that I profess; I assure you, that as I may say with Saint Paul, that I have been bred up at Gamaliel's feet (although I shall never be so arrogant as to assume to myself the rest), so I shall so far shew the effects of it, that all the world may see that no man hath or shall be ever more desirous to maintain the religion that I now profess, than I shall be.

'Now, because I am unfit for much speaking, I mean to bring up the fashion of my predecessors, to have my Lord Keeper to speak for me in most things; therefore I commanded him to speak something to you at this time; which is more for formality than for any great matter he hath to say unto you.'"

SECOND APPENDIX
THE ANCIENT REVENUE OF THE CROWN

THE significance of tonnage and poundage can only be fully understood in the light of their previous history as well as the part which they played in financing the Crown at this date. It would lead me too far from my purpose to go into any detail; but the history of tonnage and poundage may briefly be summarized thus. There were " certain sums of money, named subsidies," first of all granted for life in King Richard the Second's last parliament. From the days of King Edward the Fourth they were granted to the sovereigns for life in the earlier years of their reigns. And the act by which tonnage and poundage were granted for life to Elizabeth states that that Queen's predecessors, " time out of mind, have had and enjoyed unto them by authority of Parliament, for the defence of the same now your realm, and the keeping and safe-guard of the seas for the intercourse of merchandize, safely to come into and pass out of the same, certain sums of money, named subsidies, of all manner of goods and merchandize, coming in or going out of the same your realm "; that these subsidies were of three kinds—one subsidy, that is, called tonnage, dues levied at certain fixed rates on each " tun " of imported wine; one subsidy, also, called poundage, dues levied at certain fixed rates upon every pound sterling value of " all manner of goods and merchandizes," " carried out of this your said realm or brought into the same by way of merchandize," but subject to certain exceptions set forth in the following clause; and, finally, " one other subsidy," levied on wools and on leather. The sums to be levied are named, and the rates thus imposed were continued unchanged in the grant made to James.[1]

Not only were these " sums of money " had " time out of mind " by the Crown. An act of the same year goes further and speaks of " the sums of money paid in the name of customs and subsidies of wares and merchandizes trans-

[1] See G. W. Prothero's *Select Statutes and Other Constitutional Documents illustrative of the Reigns of Elizabeth and James I* (fourth edition, 1913), p. 26.

ported out and brought into this your Highness' realm of England by any merchant, stranger or denizen," as "an ancient revenue annexed and united to your imperial crown."[2] Such terms are profoundly significant. These subsidies went with the Crown, were inherited along with the Crown; no Crown—may we not say?—without them. From forty to fifty years later this doctrine acquired legal sanction. We come on the following passage in the judgement delivered by Clarke: "As it is not a kingdom without subjects and government, so he is not a king without revenues. . . . The revenue of the crown is the very essential part of the crown, and he who rendeth that from the King pulleth also his crown from his head, for it cannot be separated from the crown."[3] Though the words had a wider application, it follows that the Courts were at one with the Commons of Elizabeth's time in the matter of tonnage and poundage.

"One other subsidy . . . that is to say, of every merchant-denizen for every sack of wool, £1 13s. 4d." On the meaning to be placed on these words turned the question of "pretermitted customs," debated in James the First's reign. The reports in the *Journals* are, doubtless, both somewhat obscure and involved. But, unless I am wholly mistaken, the principal points were as follows. What were known as the "pretermitted customs" were duties imposed at the ports upon "cloths" manufactured from wool. Now the duties on wool were twofold: first of all, what was called "the old custom," a noble on each sack of wool; next, the "one other subsidy" mentioned in the act granting tonnage and poundage—six nobles in all to the sack. In the Statutes of Tonnage and Poundage, so the leaders of the Commons contended, certain goods were exempted by name, and among them were cloths made of wool. This exemption was, however, *from poundage*, as, indeed, was explicitly stated; and the case for the Crown rested mainly on the grant of five nobles per sack. This grant was distinct from

[2] See Prothero, *ibid.*, p. 25.
[3] In what was called Bates's case. A certain John Bates, "Turkey merchant," refused to pay the duty on currants and was sued in the Court of Exchequer. The duty, he claimed, was illegal; but judgement was given against him (November, 1606). See Prothero, *ibid.*, p. 340.

poundage, and "wool," so the Crown lawyers argued, included cloths made out of wool and had been so construed since these "customs" were first of all levied by Mary. The Commons, however, contended that "wool" could not mean woollen cloths. Moreover, the object, they argued, of levying so heavy a duty was to keep wool from being exported; it was in intention prohibitive, as we should nowadays call it. The natural conclusion was thus that it did not apply to those cloths.[4]

The sovereign from time to time issued some schedules, then called "books of rates." They determined the values of wares that were subject to the payment of dues. A new book had been issued by James, and the Commons complained of his action. This book sanctioned certain new levies, which came to be called "impositions." The King was upheld by the Courts. For the Judges in the Court of Exchequer had ruled that the King was entitled, in addition to tonnage and poundage, to levy upon exports and imports what duties soever he pleased at what rates he might care to determine. These judges could not be described as intimidated, servile, corrupt.[5]

We now see the points in dispute at the time when Charles came to the throne. We have seen how he waived them through Heath. He was ready, on those points at least, to abide by the Commons' decision and began, as we said, with *concession.*

---

[4] See the *Journals* for 1624, April 13, 16, 28. Especial attention should be paid to Heath's speech upon April 16. In particular note these remarks: "If not a duty proper for the King to ask, not to be maintained upon the Statute of Tonnage and Poundage, will disclaim to speak in it.—Edw. III a noble was given on a sack of wool by Parliament. Then clothing began in England. Then thought fit to give the King an equal profit. 21 Edw. IV. a noble upon six cloths given:—VI. —14d. Then the Statute of Tonnage gives five nobles.—I. This 40s. belongs to the King, out of wool. Queen Mary's time, and before, less than 40s. taken, and yet more than a noble.—Unjust, to take more than a noble, as well as 40s. Not screwed up to the height, but a part pretermitted; hence the denomination. For the ground of it, must resort to the Statute. A clause in the Statute gives it:—'One other subsidy, for every sack of wool, five nobles.' If these words cannot reach to cloth, then the King no right to this custom." The speaker appeals *to a statute.*

[5] See p. 172, *supra,* note 2.

THIRD APPENDIX

FOUR versions exist of this message, and, as its contents are important, I set them down here for the reader. The *Lords' Journals* have these two entries. On July the 4th in the morning, " The Lord Keeper signified unto the Lords, that he had a message to deliver them from the King: *videlicet,* ' that his Majesty, considering the great danger of the infection at this time (whereof he is more sensible in respect of this assembly than of his own particular), will put an end to this session as soon as he shall understand of their readiness for the same; and that this be signified unto the Commons.' Agreed, to be signified unto them at the conference touching the Petition " (the petition concerning religion). On July the 4th *post meridiem,* " Being returned, and the House resumed; the Lord Keeper reported, that first he delivered unto the Commons the message from the King, touching his Majesty's sorrow for the great danger they were in, by reason of the sickness; and that his Majesty is ready to make an end of the session when he shall understand that they are ready to have an end." [1] In the *Commons' Journals* also we read under July the 4th *post meridiem*: " Sir Edw. Coke reporteth from the conference.—That the Lord Keeper said, he had lately received a message from the King to the Lords and Commons. That the King had taken into his consideration our safety, yea, more than his own. That the sickness strongly increased: that therefore, when we [' we ' should presumably be ' he '] should hear the Commons ready (for we [this again must be ' he '] would not hasten us in any thing) he would put an end to this sitting." [2] The *Fawsley Debates* have this entry: " At a conference with the Lords the same day. My Lord Keeper delivered a message from the King. That his Majesty took in his consideration and care our safety,

---

[1] *Lords' Journals,* III, pp. 453, 454.
[2] *Commons' Journals,* I, p. 802.

more than his own, the sickness strongly increasing; when he should receive word that we were ready, yet not pressing us to any haste but such as we should think fit, he would not defer to make an end of this session by his presence, or otherwise." [3] No reference whatever, be it noted, is made to the subsidies bill. We have seen what Sir John Coke declared in the Commons on July the 8th.[4] Then Conway on July 11 " signified unto the Lords, ' that his Majesty takes knowledge of the two subsidies now granted unto him, which he doth most graciously accept of; but the necessities of the present affairs are such that they cannot rest there, but their further counsels are to be had therein.' " [5]

[3] *Fawsley Debates*, p. 41.
[4] See p. 42, *supra*.
[5] *Lords' Journals*, III, p. 464.

FOURTH APPENDIX

THE BISHOP OF MENDE TO RICHELIEU

THE Keeper of the MSS., British Museum, very kindly supplied me with the following, for which I am greatly indebted, in reply to some inquiries I made on September 10, 1926 : " Mr. Cooke is correct in supposing that the three foot-notes in vol. v. of Gardiner's *Hist. of England,* 1603–1642, which he mentions in his letter of the 10th inst., refer to *two* letters from the Bishop of Mende to Cardinal Richelieu ; the letters, however, are not both of the same date. The position is as follows : (a) Gard. p. 415, n. 2. The actual passage is in King's MS. 137, f. 38b. Gardiner has quoted the old page number of the beginning of the letter (p. 84, which is now f. 37b). The letter was received on 25[= 15] Aug. 1625. (b) Gard. p. 418, n. 1. The reference in Gardiner is wrong, for the passage in question is found in the letter beginning on the old page 99 (now f. 45), and not in the letter previously described. This letter was received on 29[= 19] August 1625, as Gardiner correctly states. (c) Gard. p. 429, n. 3. The reference is to the same letter as (b) above, the old page number being now correctly given. The actual passage occurs on f. 46. Mr. Cooke is also correct in thinking that Gardiner obtained from King's MS. 137 the date of the Council meeting only and not his account of the proceedings. The passage is as follows : ' Bouquingan [Buckingham] donc se voiant trompé en son dessein et que pour avoir sacriffiés les Catholiques il n'estoit point a Couvert, il fit assembler le Conseil a Ortford [Oxford] le jeudy suivant ou resolution fut prise de rompre le dit Parlement sans avoir Esgard a la necessité de leurs affaires Le Vendredy au matin ; et le Roy apres leur avoir declaré par son Garde des Seaux que Bouquingan n'avoit rien fait que par son expres Commandem^t il leur fit enjoindre de se retirer en leurs Maisons.' Thursday was 11th August, and the passage confirms Gardiner's statement that the Council was held on that day. It may be pointed out that either the writer or the copyist of the letter in King's MS. 137, f. 45 was in error in giving the date of the earlier Council meeting as ' Le lundy 19° de ce mois ' : Monday was the 18th [= 8th] August, and this fact may possibly clear up the difficulty of Gard. p. 418, n. 1."